TABLE OF CONTENTS

FOREWORD

I first met Ken Beaton the first time I hosted a *Fast Track To Cash Flow* event in Ottawa back in 2003. Over the years that I have known him, Ken has become one of my biggest supporters. He started out as an event attendee, then quickly became an event volunteer (with his lovely wife, Joanne) and when I found out how successful and creative Ken had become with his real estate investments, I asked him to be one of my expert speakers.

Over the last few years, Ken has become one of the most popular contributing writers to the *Fast Track Inner Circle* membership program. Between his articles and his speaking at our events, Ken has proven himself to be a true 'teacher' (in the best sense of the word). He absolutely loves to show new real estate investors how to get started and avoid the many pitfalls of real estate investing.

I consider Ken to be one of the most creative Canadian investors I know, always striving to make every deal a win-win for both sides. He is honest, operates with integrity, and is passionate about real estate and helping people learn to invest!

Dave Dubeau is another gentleman I have come to know very well over the last few years. When I first met him, he was in the midst of his 'creative' real estate investing career – flipping 18 houses in 18 months. That alone qualifies him in my mind as an expert in creative real estate investing.

But Dave's real talent lies in marketing, and in the years since he began working with my company as my main 'marketing guy' he has helped me immensely to grow *Fast Track to Cash Flow* to where it is today.

So if you are interested in learning how to invest creatively in Real Estate, and purchase your first rental property, or your hundred and first, I highly recommend that you read this book with a pen in hand – taking lots of notes as you go!

See you at the top!

Darren Weeks
Founder, Fast Track to Cash Flow Inc.

About the Authors

Ken Beaton

Ken Beaton eats, breathes, and sleeps real estate – it's his passion! He has gone from an operator of a seasonal resort in 1985 to President of his own company, ARCA Real Estate Investments Inc. The discovery of Robert Kiyosaki's book *Rich Dad, Poor Dad* unleashed Ken's passion for real estate and teaching, and transformed his life. He's contributed to *Rich Dad*'s educational program and mentored more than 100 successful real estate investors. But he's most famous for his 'Creative Real Estate' deals; when he sees an opportunity he loves to ask, "How CAN I make this work?"

Ken is a regular speaker at Darren Weeks' events as well as a long-time contributor to Weeks' *Fast Track Inner Circle Newsletter.* Over the past eight years, Ken and the love of his life, Joanne, have purchased millions of dollars of real estate and now own more than 100 doors. He and Joanne are now working on a new seniors' building for affordable housing.

For a copy of Ken's *Real Estate Analyzer,* or to see the analyzer in use, visit **www.realestatefirsttimers.com** and for more information about Ken and his company, visit **www.arcarealestate.ca**

Dave Dubeau

Dave Dubeau began his infatuation with marketing while living in San Jose, Costa Rica. By learning and implementing effective direct response marketing he took his start-up company from the bottom to the top three in 2.5 years.

When Dave returned to Canada in 2003, he put his marketing skills to good use, first in the fields of 'Creative Real Estate Investing,' where he did '18 flips in 18 months', then with an advertising business and later as a marketing consultant.

But Dave came into his own as a bona-fide marketing expert when he began working with Canadian *Rich Dad* Darren Weeks. Together they created the *Fast Track Inner Circle* Membership Program, and Dave eventually became the "Marketing Guy" for Darren's Fast Track Group of Companies.

Dave's company, appropriately called Results Enterprises Inc., is based out of Kamloops, British Columbia, Canada. His website is **www.resultsenterprises.com**

Introduction

The purpose of this book is to provide the beginning investor – let's call him or her a 'property virgin' – the means and the opportunity to play the real estate game. We'll show you how to not just to push or shove your way in, but to do it the right way, so that your initial investment will continue to generate cash in good times and bad.

At the same time, we will debunk the myths about real estate investing, separating fact from fiction. We will not only expose the lies, but also show you how to find the perfect team to help you reach your goals, discover the best deals, and figure out whether they are lucrative or not. But that's not all, we will also explain how to make an offer, close the deal, and manage your property, because finding the right renters – rather than tenants from hell – is critical for a landlord.

Of course, we will not overlook that all-important bottom line – using your properties to create a passive income. On these pages, you will also find advice on how to buy lots of real estate with none of your own money, and learn *the* number one creative real estate strategy – and no, it is not the usual 'buy and hold'! And, in addition to all that, we will show you where to look when you are ready to take your investments to the next level. By the time you finish reading, you will know what steps to take – and what pitfalls to avoid – to buy your very first property.

Now, you might be asking yourself, "Why should I listen to these guys? What makes them such hotshot real estate investors?"

These are very legitimate questions, so let us tell you a bit about ourselves.

Ken Beaton:

I have a civil engineering technology degree. That in itself doesn't make me a real estate expert, except that I used to own and operate a seasonal resort (a fancy name for a campground), managing 100 tenants.

I eventually sold that business because it wasn't as profitable as I had hoped. However, one of the jobs I had at that time was as a real estate agent, and that position opened doors – no pun intended – to buying and selling properties. Unfortunately for me, those operations were done the old, conventional way. I was bursting with innovative ideas and tried to introduce all kinds of creative strategies into the mix. Not surprisingly, I kept hitting brick walls. Everyone was saying, "You can't do that," "That's illegal," and the litany of other "can'ts" and "don'ts". Frustrated, I left the industry, focusing on honing my sales skills. I started selling Park Model trailers at the campground, which re-sparked my interest in creative real estate. I finally sold that business, took a year off, and learned everything I could not only about real estate per se, but also about how to apply my creativity and out-of-the box thinking to this industry. My life has not been the same since.

Since 2001, I have been an active (and very successful) real estate developer. I currently own more than 100 properties worth millions.

Before I started investing, my learning curve was pretty high, so I had to learn. All that education was not free. In the first year alone, I probably spent at least $60,000 on courses, travel, etc. Over time, it added up to $100,000. I took a lot of courses, which included a mentor at the end of the program. I did everything the mentor told me to do, and I think he was impressed with my performance because he offered me a position mentoring his other students.

In the meantime, I was buying up properties left and right. I'd estimate that 60% of the real estate I now own – 75 doors – were purchased during that time.

I might add that as I was mentoring students – over 100 in all – I also continued to deepen my own knowledge. My education encompassed not only real estate, but also self-development, which proved to be a very valuable skill for myself and for others. I continue the one-on-one, personal mentoring to this day. This means that I go to a student's residence, sit down with him or her for three solid days, and then come up with a killer plan.

I suppose all of the above points answer the question of why I am qualified to write this book!

Dave Dubeau:

Yes, Ken is eminently qualified to give real estate investment advice, and not only because he has been working with Canadian *Rich Dad* Darren Weeks for the last several years.

Ken often participates in our events and is a very popular speaker because of the quality of his content, as well as his generosity in sharing his knowledge and experience with all of us. I interviewed Ken at length about his winning strategies any first-time investor can use. His answers constitute the content of this book.

As for myself, I have nowhere near the level of expertise Ken has, though I do have a lot of creative real estate experience as well. I am originally from British Columbia, lived in San José, Costa Rica for 11 years, and moved back to Canada in 2003 with my Costa Rica-born wife and two children.

In Costa Rica I ran a language training school. I enjoyed it, but when I returned to Canada I wanted to try something different. I came across Ron LeGrande, a creative real estate guru. I bought all his courses, investing probably in the $10,000-$15,000 range in my education. My claim to fame is doing 18 flips in 18 months in British Columbia.

Experience in the creative side of real estate is great, but what I happened to be extremely good at was generating deal flow. What exactly does that mean? It means having deals come to *me*. The way I did that was through marketing specifically for real estate. I must be a very good marketer because deals just kept coming to me. That, in a nutshell, is my background.

We hope you will find this book extremely useful and possibly even entertaining. But please, keep in mind that we are real estate investors, not legal experts. We know as much about law as we do about quantum physics – possibly less. So please, before you embark on any deals or transactions outlined in this book, follow any suggestion or advice, before you jump in with both feet, seek proper legal and accounting advice from an accredited professional who knows the laws in your area. Ken is based in Ontario and I am in British Columbia. If you're in a different province, some details might vary slightly, but the concepts in general apply anywhere.

Intrigued? Well then, turn the page.

CHAPTER 1

WHY REAL ESTATE?

Or, more precisely, why real estate is the number one investment choice Canadians should make

As you will see throughout this book, security and profitability are certainly among the most compelling reasons why real estate is the number one investment choice Canadians should make.

Simply put, real estate is not only lucrative, but is also one of the safest investments out there if purchased and managed properly. It is so secure that even in a slumping economy, you will see your net worth increase if you buy real estate properly. In fact, I don't know anybody – myself included - who invested in real estate wisely and has not made a bundle.

That's why 80% of the world's richest people – Donald Trump is one example – hold their wealth in real estate. They know it is a low risk way to generate cash and create a reliable safety net for themselves and their families. Once you retire and need to supplement your pension, real estate will be a great source of ongoing passive income. And you can take out some of the equity as well.

Having said that, please keep in mind that I am talking about building *long-term* wealth, not a flash-in-the-pan, get-rich-quick scheme that may – or may not – generate immediate cash, but in all likelihood will not withstand recessionary trends. However, in this book we will cover all sorts of different profit centres, and in one of the chapters we will talk about a very creative real estate strategy that can generate nice chunks of change in your pocket fairly quickly – if you use the right tools.

Ready to become a full-time real estate investor?

Congratulations, you made the right choice. By now you are aware of some of the 'pros' of real estate investing, as outlined above – and we will focus on them again and again. However, there are also 'cons' you should consider before quitting your job and becoming a full-time real estate investor.

First of all, this venture does require hands-on work. Though we refer to real estate as passive income, and there is certainly an element of passiveness to it, you do have to actively manage your properties. Even if you hire someone else to do this for you, you still have to keep an eye on the operations because there is always that risk of an unforeseeable problem creeping up. For example, I once 'inherited' some Hell's Angels as tenants in one of the properties I purchased. Or, there is always a possibility that someone is not paying rent on time, or maybe partying all night and disturbing the neighbours.

Whatever the problem, you as the owner have to be on top of it. Management know-how is fine, but people skills are also very useful. If you don't have those skill sets, then make sure you hire someone who does.

Secondly, dealing with all of the above problems, and whatever else might come up, can be discouraging and frustrating at times, especially since your profits are on the line. However, that's the nature of running your own business. It's not for the faint of heart, but at the end of the day it's so worth it. I, for one, would do it again in a heartbeat.

Now that you have been fore-warned, let's talk about six 'profit centres' a beginning investor like you should know about.

Profit centre number 1: Appreciation

The first one is appreciation of your properties. In simplest terms, say you buy a property for $100,000 and several years later sell it for $150,000. You made a nice profit because the property value has appreciated by $50,000 during the time you owned it. However, I must admit this is one of my pet peeves because so many people, especially novice investors, buy a piece of real estate with only the idea of appreciation in mind, and I don't call that investing; I call that speculating. We are going to show you how to make money with real estate even if the value of your property stays flat.

Profit centre number 2: Instant equity

The second profit centre is instant equity; in other words, you make money as soon as you buy a property. A quick and easy example to illustrate this point is that every house that's listed (unless you are in a really hot sellers' market), you will get for at least 5% below market value. That 5% is instant equity that can go to your net worth statement. Translated into raw numbers, let's say you purchase a house that's on the market for $200,000 for

$190,000. With no effort on your part, you have created a $10,000 instant equity.

Once you get good at understanding how the game works and learn some basic negotiation skills, you can easily find properties way below market value.

Now, you may be wondering why anyone would sell a house for 5% – or even as much as 30% or 40% – below market value. Typically, the owners are highly motivated to sell quickly – for example, they are going through a divorce and neither spouse wants the other to get more money, so they are playing off each other. Or maybe the owners have to move because of a job transfer. Non-payment of mortgage and fear of foreclosure are also big motivators to unload the property quickly. And by the way, don't be put off by the condition of a run-down house, provided you get it way, way below market value. All it takes is a bit of lipstick and hard work to turn it around, and that instant equity is staring you in the face.

Profit centre number 3: Depreciation

Profit centre number three is depreciation. It may sound negative, but, in fact, it is not. We are blessed in our country because the government will allow us to depreciate a piece of property even though typically it appreciates in value. In a sense, we appreciate depreciation.

Let me explain, and I'll just give you a big picture. Let's say you own a 20-year-old house. What the government is saying is that as the house gets older, it will have problems, be it a leaky roof, the hot water tank on the blink, or the overall structure getting weaker. The government allows you to take part of the value of the building and lower it year by year – this is called depreciation. Some people refer to that as phantom money or deferred savings because when you do sell that property, you are going to have to pay the savings portion back to the government.

In Canada, you are allowed to depreciate the property 4% annually; whatever the portion of the total cost was attributed to the building, that's what you can depreciate. As an example, let's take a house with a market value of $200,000. The dirt is worth $50,000 and the structure $150,000. The replacement value of the building is $150,000. So the government is going to say you can take that value of the building and lower it by 4% a year (which equals $6000 in year 1) until it's down to 0. However, I suggest that you seek the advice of your accountant on whether to use this particular option for tax purposes.

Profit centre number 4: Cash flow

In the investment world, we say that cash flow – i.e. your monthly profit – is king. This means you should never buy any property if it isn't cash flow positive. Even if you live in Vancouver, you can still make cash flow positive if you get the rents, but there are definitely more difficult markets, and you do not want to get into a negative cash flow situation. Even if the property is not generating any cash flow, at least you are breaking even – your tenants are paying your mortgage and all your expenses, and you can count on your property's appreciation.

Here's an example of cash flow: Let's say you have a tenant in your rental property and he is paying $1000 a month. At the end of the day, after you deduct all of your expenses, including mortgage, taxes, and everything else (I'll explain later what all the main expenses are), you have a $50 profit left over – that is positive cash flow.

Naturally, you want to get investment properties that are positive cash flow, and that's what we're really going to be pushing in this book – how to buy your first investment property and have it be a positive cash flow property. So whether you live in downtown Toronto or downtown Vancouver, you are going to be able to do this. On the other hand, if you are not able to do it with the house, the condo, or the apartment next door, you may just have to go to the suburbs. Find an area that will work for you.

Profit centre number 5: Leverage

This is where the bank will lend you money to buy the property, so you can leverage a $10,000 down payment and the bank will typically lend you 95%. What this means is that if you buy a $200,000 property, you can control it with as little as $10,000.

The benefit of appreciation is a perfect example here. If you take that $10,000, put it into the stock market and get 3% interest, you are going to earn $300. But if you take that same $10,000 and invest it in a piece of real estate that appreciates at the same 3%, it's earning 3% of $200,000.

So you've earned $6,000 of appreciation on $10,000, which is a 60% return on your investment in one year. Let's see: $300 versus $6,000. You be the judge.

Let it suffice to say that leverage is one of the biggest advantages of real estate, since you are controlling this huge asset with very little of your own money, so your cash-on-cash return is huge.

Profit centre number 6: Principal reduction

What we're talking about here is the financing of the property. When you get a mortgage from a bank, a portion of each monthly payment goes to the interest and a portion goes to the principal pay down. At the beginning, 95-96% of your first payment is going to go to interest. Over the course of that year, you are going to reduce the principal amount by approximately 4%. That principal reduction is what we call phantom cash because you don't actually see that money in your profit but the debt is being reduced by 4%, so you have to include that in your taxable income.

For example, let's say you bought the $200,000 property with 10% down, so you have a mortgage for $180,000. After your tenant pays rent and you pay your mortgage, at the end of the year you will have paid that mortgage principal down by 4%, which roughly translates to $7000. This means your equity in the property has increased by $7000, so that's another profit centre. In essence, your tenant is paying your mortgage for you.

Profit Summary

Now, if we take a conservative view and go with a 3% appreciation that is an average in Canada right now, this is what we get: A $200,000 property purchased a year ago is now worth $206,000, so you have already earned $6,000 on the investment through appreciation. You also have instant equity, because you bought that $200,000 property for 5% below market value, shelling out $190,000 for a $200,000 property. As you saw under Profit Centre number 2, this is totally doable. Instant equity of $10,000 plus appreciation of $6,000 provides you with $16,000 in equity.

The $6000 tax benefit for depreciation could translate into a $2000 tax savings on your income tax return, dependent on your personal tax situation.

What about cash flow? Since we are being conservative, let's say $50 a month times 12 equals $600. Admittedly, that's not a very sexy sum, but keep in mind that you have leverage – in other words, you used the bank's money to buy the property in the first place.

Let's look at principal reduction using the above example again. The $7,000 principal reduction is an increase in the property equity and your personal net worth.

And the good news is....

If you followed our math, you'll see that we got $6000 in appreciation, $10,000 in instant equity, $6000 in depreciation (approximately a $2000 tax savings), $600 in positive cash flow, and $7000 in principal pay down. All that money is generated by the property in which you invested only $10,000 – that's a hefty 256% return on your investment if you include the depreciation. All in all, not too shabby, is it?

Notes & Thoughts!

CHAPTER 2

HOW THE GAME WORKS

Or seven real estate myths you should never, ever believe

As a novice investor, you will undoubtedly hear numerous half-truths and outright lies about how to make money in real estate. Problem is, a lot of what you come across is just baseless mumbo-jumbo. How do you separate fact from fiction so that you can make informed decisions about your investments? Read on.

Myth number 1: You need a lot of money to get started in real estate.

Not! What you do need is *access* to money, but the great thing is it doesn't have to be *your* money! Did you ever hear of OPM? This is an acronym for 'other people's money'. Here's the beauty of it: Everybody thinks that no-money-down deals don't exist. The reality is they do exist, but it's virtually impossible to get these kinds of deals with a bank. But private financing is definitely an option.

Fact is, you can use OPM and get the bank to do the mortgage. As long as the down payment is getting paid by somebody, the bank will be happy, and even if you use your own line of credit, this will be a no-money-down deal. You might think it's your line of credit so it's not really a no-money-down, but it's the bank's money, and it is lending it to you to provide the down payment.

So the message to remember is you don't have to be a millionaire to buy multiple properties. Even if you are broke or in debt, you can still buy properties, as long as you can show other people why it's worthwhile for them to invest with you.

Myth number 2: You need a bank to do real estate

Again, that's a no. It always amazes me how many people still think that they have to go to a bank to get a mortgage or a loan, and that mortgage brokers cost money, etc. Really, there's nothing further from the truth. When you go to a bank, you are dealing with just one bank, one lender, so you narrow down your choices. But if you go to a mortgage broker and you choose the broker correctly, you will have access to over 50 different lenders across the country, including the top five banks. And the beauty of it is you don't have to pay for their services; the banks or the lending facility will pay them their commission for any new residential mortgage.

All this to say that you don't have to have your local banker in your back pocket; in fact, I suggest you don't deal with your bank at all, but get a good mortgage broker who can find you the best deal.

Myth number 3: You have to use a realtor

Quite often people think I am slamming real estate agents, but it's not true. I used to be a real estate agent myself, so I know how the game works. I know the limited amount of training they receive in order to do the job that they do, and they are not necessarily the best qualified individuals to represent you in a deal at all times.

Fact is, there are good real estate agents and bad real estate agents. You need to do your homework and find the best one for you. Later in the book, we'll talk about how to do that. But you really don't need one to do a deal; in fact, there are definite advantages to working directly with the seller. One-on-one with the seller allows you to have control over the negotiating process and make sure it goes the way you want it. With a realtor, you sometimes end up dealing with more than one intermediary before your offer is passed on to the seller. This can create a situation for miscommunication and your original idea or request might get distorted and your control goes out the window.

The other myth is that when you deal with a real estate agent, you can't get to the seller directly. That too is not true, though a lot of agents will tell you it's not allowed or it's illegal. You have an opportunity and a legal right to make a presentation to the seller, and if you can't get to the seller, you can add a personalized cover letter explaining what you want and who you are. You always have to try to get to the seller in some way, shape or form. If you can sit down face-to-face with the seller and work out the deal yourself, then you can get the realtor to write it up for you. Now, it's very likely that the realtor or the listing agent will not look kindly on your desire to establish a direct relationship with the seller, but there's nothing actually stopping you from knocking on the seller's door on your own. Many agents fear that they will lose a potential sale if they allow you direct contact with the seller so you need to assure the agent that this is not the case and you still need their services.

Myth number 4: Professional real estate investors are slumlords, or you have to become a slumlord to make money in this business

Some friends jokingly call me a slumlord, but this notion is a total fabrication. Yes, there are slumlords out there, just as there are unscrupulous people in any business, but you don't have to become one to make money in real estate. I strive to provide affordable and clean housing for my tenants – the kind of housing I wouldn't mind living in myself. A related myth is that professional real estate invest-ors are sharks preying on little old ladies or ripping off poor families going into foreclosure.

True, there are some sharks out there. You get all types. But certainly, you don't have to be dishonest or unethical to make money in this business. I am a perfect example of that – I am easy going, never pressure anyone, have a good reputation, and yet have become very successful.

Myth number 5: Real estate investing is all about getting rich quick

Of course there are real estate investors who make a hell of a lot of money quickly, but they tend to be higher risk takers, totally uneducated, or just plain lucky. They are the ones who are playing the speculation game, and that's extremely risky. The good news is that you can make a lot of money in real estate through other, less risky methods, but you have to be patient. I am speaking as someone who currently owns over 100 units worth millions, but I haven't created all that wealth overnight. This book does not teach you a get-rich-quick scheme; rather, you will learn how to build long-term wealth starting with your first property, and do it slow and steady.

Myth number 6: It's a seller's market, so don't go looking for deals

That's definitely a myth. I originally found it hard to believe that somebody would be willing to sell their property at 30%, 40%, or even 50% below market value. But the reality is they are out there and it doesn't matter if it's a seller's market or a buyer's market, it happens all the time. It will just happen more often during a buyer's market. Other deals can be found due to people's life changes, such as sellers who are divorcing or moving and are motivated to sell quickly. Or there are properties that are totally mismanaged or neglected, and other opportunities out there that will sell well below market value as well.

Myth number 7: Real estate is too risky

Define 'risky' for me. Putting all your money in the stock market and watching it tank by 30% in a couple of days, that's pretty risky. Risky is putting all your money in mutual funds and getting whacked by the fees.

People may think real estate is risky because they see those who are just speculating with real estate. You can get your butt burned in speculation. So if the only thing you are focusing on is appreciation with your investment, the quick buck, a flip or something like that, then yes, it can be risky.

Education is the key factor here. Learn about how to invest safely and see your profits multiply.

Notes & Thoughts!

Chapter 3

Your Power Team

Before we talk about all the different people who should become part of your power team, we need to touch on why a team is important in the first place. Many self-employed business people have what may be referred to as 'the lone ranger syndrome', meaning they want to do everything themselves, either because they think other people are incompetent or they don't want to pay money for services they believe they can do themselves.

That is not a smart way to run your real estate business. Fact is, you need to create a team because the more people you have helping you, the more you can focus on your highest value activities, such as finding and negotiating deals. All the secondary activities are best delegated to others.

In real estate, you can't do it all alone. And if you want to be surrounded by competent people, you can't be cheap in what you are willing to pay them for their services. I speak from personal experience here – I used to go with the lowest price, but I quickly learned that the rock-bottom price doesn't always give you value for your money. I am not suggesting you should choose the most expensive contractor either, but you do have to be ready and willing to pay a fair price for services provided to you.

The people you won't be able to live without

No, it's not your spouse or significant other, though of course they are very important people in your life. I am talking about team members who will be essential to you as you get started and grow your business.

First is a good realtor. In the previous chapter, I said you don't really need a realtor, but you are probably going to use one for your first deal to help walk you through the process. Obviously, if you are going to use a realtor, get a good one. So let's talk about what a good realtor does for you and what qualities you should look for.

There's a saying that you don't know what you don't know. An experienced and qualified realtor will guide you and show you the way. How do you find a good one? It should preferably be someone who has experience in buying properties for themselves; in other words, your realtor should also be a real estate investor.

Now, you may be thinking, "Why would I want to work with another investor, who might grab all the deals for himself?" Good point, but the fact is that not all the deals that are out there are good for the realtor; on the other hand, they may be perfect for you. Or perhaps the realtor is interested in the property but is strapped for cash and has no clue how to use OPM – other people's money – so he has to let it go. That property will then land right in your lap.

Of course, just because a deal comes your way and the realtor doesn't grab it for himself, doesn't necessarily mean that particular property is good for you. This is where you should use due diligence.

An advantage of working with a realtor who is also a successful investor is that he will have the expertise to help analyze whether a particular property is a good deal and show you the numbers. At the end of the day, however, you will have to make the decision yourself.

And it doesn't really matter whether the realtor has been in business six years or six months. What's important is what he knows and how good his negotiating skills are. How do you go about finding that person? Go to the manager's office, explain your needs, and they will hopefully direct you to the right person. Another possibility is to ask successful investors whom they work with and then go and interview that realtor.

"What should you expect of a good realtor?" is a logical question. He will make sure you don't pay too much. He will also have all the necessary resources to find good properties for you. Realtors have access to Multiple Listing Service (MLS), but they can also locate good deals before they are listed on MLS.

Also, a surprising number of vendors don't want their property listed on MLS, and a lot of agents will have what they call 'pocket listings' that never make it to the market. So, they are a great resource to find properties for you.

A word of caution: Though realtors may bring you lots of deals, not all of them will be hot deals, so you do have to be careful. Also, they may not negotiate effectively on your behalf, and here we go back to the advice in a previous chapter: Try to establish a relationship directly with the seller. If you can't have a face-to-face meeting with the vendor, at least include a cover letter with your offer explaining who you are and why you are interested in the property.

By the way, you have to understand how realtors work and how they get paid. Since they get paid by the seller, they are legally obliged to represent the seller's interests. They are under contract to represent you as well, so keep your cards close to your chest, don't divulge information even to your own personal agent that you don't want going back to the seller. For example, don't say upfront how much you are prepared to pay.

Quite often you will go to an open house and you will be talking to a listing agent, and the listing agent will say something to the effect of, "Oh, I think you can buy it for this price," when it's actually listed at a much higher price. What they are doing, technically, may not be illegal, but it's certainly unethical, as they are not representing the seller properly. Normally, the seller should not be telling the agent how much they're willing to go down, just like the purchaser should not be telling an agent how much they're willing to pay for the property. So keep that information to yourself.

Another thing to keep under wraps is this: For negotiating, generally speaking, you ask for everything, but if you don't expect anything, don't tell your agent that. Keep emotions and thoughts to yourself; if the agent senses that you are enthusiastic about the property, they will be like sharks smelling blood in the water, and will go in for the kill.

Another thing a realtor won't do for you is legal work. And that brings us to another important member of your team – a notary public or a lawyer.

Your legal team

If you are a new investor, I would suggest that any offer you make is reviewed by your lawyer or notary. They can make sure you haven't put a clause in there that's going to be harmful to you. They are not going to provide advice such as whether you are paying too much or anything of that nature, they just want to make sure that there's not a clause in there that's going to screw up your financing or put you at risk. So that's the first thing. The second thing is they are going to make sure that everything is legal. They are going to do some researching on the property to ensure that what you are buying is what you are getting, and everything is in good standing, there are no outstanding liens, no hidden information relating to that property, etc. They will also help with financing, representing you and your bank or your lender in creating a mortgage for that property. They do all the paperwork necessary to close the deal.

What they won't do is tell you what the value of the property is, or give you advice on whether the property in question is a good deal for you.

The funny thing is they will tell you if the deal seems to be risky – for example, if you are taking out a second mortgage or something like that. Their role is to point out all of the potential pitfalls that they can see, but not to tell you what a smoking good deal this is.

A word of advice here: When hiring a lawyer, make sure you choose someone who specializes in real estate. Don't go to a jack-of-all-trades or someone practicing in another field of law – go to someone who has experience in real estate.

The same tip I gave you before regarding finding a realtor would apply here as well. Ask for recommendations and resist the urge to go to the cheapest attorney or notary around. Remember the old saying, 'you get what you pay for'. Saving money at the onset may cost you more money in the end, when it becomes clear that the person you hired for next to nothing really is worth next to nothing.

Just as with a realtor, finding a lawyer who is also a real estate investor can be beneficial to you (and generally speaking, all your power team members should understand the game of investing in real estate).

A home inspector is a must

Team member number three is a property inspector. Even a novice investor knows that he or she should never buy property – even a brand new one – without a professional inspection.

Depending on where you live, finding a reliable home inspector may be a challenge, because different provinces have their own rules and regulations. I do know that anyone can go to a local community college and sign up for courses which teach you how to become a property inspector. Anyone could do that and learn the theory, but they may have no on-the-job, practical experience. So it's always best to follow recommendations from other investors or from real estate agents who have used different inspectors and know who the good ones are and who to avoid. Keep in mind too that inspections are quite superficial; inspectors can't go digging into walls and crawl spaces, but they will help identify a lot of minor issues and potential big issues as well.

As with other professions mentioned above, here too resist the urge to hire an inspector on the cheap side. It won't be in your best interest.

Money, money, money

You won't get far as an investor without money, so finding the 'money person' (let's call him or her a 'financier') is crucial. So is the selection process – you don't want to do this at the last minute, and you certainly don't want to just pull this one out of the phone book.

Occasionally, you might have to borrow money from the bank, but personally I am of the belief that you should use a mortgage broker for your loans. The biggest difference is that this strategy gives you options and flexibility, and a mortgage broker has access to over 50 different lenders across the country, including private money.

Here again beware, because there are good and not so good mortgage brokers, and even though all these people have access to a lot of different lenders, it doesn't necessarily mean they can find you money at an advantageous rate. And some will have dubious business practices, so be careful. Make sure that the information that's being provided both to the broker and from the broker is legitimate, because if the lender comes back a year later and it's the wrong information, you will be responsible, not the broker.

One question to ask your broker is if he or she has access to a hard moneylender, and if so, how many? 'Hard money' means private funds, usually a wealthy person with lots of cash that can be lent, or access to money they can borrow at a low interest rate, and lend to you at a much higher interest rate so they profit off the spread.

In a way, these people act as their own banks but they are willing to overlook a lot of things that the banks won't; in return for that, if it's a higher risk property and you are more needy, the interest rate is going to be considerably higher. You can be paying anywhere from 12%-18% for private money, and they like to be paid a small percentage as a finder's fee up front as well. Mortgage Brokers also have access to what we call subprime lenders. Subprime lenders are a great resource to have available, though subprime has a bad reputation right now due to recent events in the banking industry. But these lenders will lend to riskier individuals or riskier projects and in exchange they charge a higher interest rate than the more conventional lenders would.

So what will a good mortgage broker do for you? He will look at your deal and, from his experience – which is why you need to have an experienced broker, not a greenhorn – he will decide who the top five lenders are who he should send this deal to. He will try to get you the best rates available out there. Again, this is why you want to go on a reference or a referral basis in order to find one of these individuals. Look for somebody who has worked for other investors and is an investor himself so he understands what you are trying to do, and will keep you legal.

On the other hand, no mortgage broker – at least not an honest one – will guarantee that he will find you sources of financing. Also, he can't always get you the rate of return or the interest rate you are hoping to achieve. But overall, mortgage brokers are better than banks because of their flexibility and available options.

Those are the four core members of your team that you really can't – and shouldn't – do without. You will probably find that as your business grows, you will also need different types of lawyers for different properties, an accountant and a bookkeeper, property managers, and handy men.

Whenever I go looking at a new area to invest in, especially if it's in another town, one of the first things I look for are property management teams and handy man services. If I can't find those services, I am not interested in buying in that location, regardless of how good the deal is.

Then, of course, there are mentors, advisors, and people you can bounce ideas off – all excellent resources for your team as well. Bottom line: Trustworthy and reliable people on your team will be of great value to you.

Notes & Thoughts!

CHAPTER 4

FINDING THE DEAL

In previous chapters, we talked about why real estate is the right investment for everybody, how the real estate game really works, and who you need to have on your real estate power team. Now we will talk about how to actually get your first property.

Before you start thinking about what kind of property you want to buy and in what location, consider what you would like to achieve with your real estate investment. Do you want a huge portfolio or just a few properties? If it's the latter, you don't have to go into the low-end of town where it's going to be high maintenance with the tenants. You are going to find some really good deals there, but it might be too overwhelming for a beginner. So take a look at the neighbourhoods and decide where you want to invest. You don't necessarily want to invest in the high-end of town because you are probably not going to achieve positive cash flow. Even in the middle-class area, it's going to be difficult to achieve positive cash flow, so you are looking to get into a high-low end or a low-middle neighbourhood. You can identify these neighbourhoods by just driving around with a map of that particular town. Identify the areas of interest, and then see your real estate agent, who will help you look for properties in that area.

Different residential options

There are several real estate market options available: Single-family homes, and multi-units such as a duplex, triplex and fourplex. As soon as you go beyond a fourplex, your financing rules change, so no need to be overly ambitious with your first venture – stick to a single, duplex or triplex to start with.

Let's focus on what is reasonable for a newbie investor: Detached single-family homes, apartments/condos, as well as single units in a duplex or a triplex.

When my good friend, *Canadian Rich Dad* Darren Weeks was a young guy just getting started with no money in his pocket, he liked to focus on condos. He bought a couple of dozen condominiums in condo complexes because there was less maintenance and, theoretically, less maintenance costs. In a multi-condo unit if something went wrong with the furnace, the roof, or anything else, it was taken care of by the condo corporation.

Whatever kind of property you purchase, be aware of not only the advantages it offers, but also the disadvantages.

Let's start with a single-family detached house. For this kind of dwelling, you are responsible for everything yourself. On the flip side, you don't have anybody imposing rules and regulations on you as you would in a condo corporation.

When you get into a semi-detached residence, you are now sharing a portion of the common areas. It's a good way for developers to cut costs by putting more properties on less space. The downside is that the proximity to your neighbour is much closer and you can have potential issues. If you get a tenant in your place who doesn't get along with the neighbour next door, you will have problems.

Condominiums too come with their own list of pros and cons. A definite pro is that you don't have to worry about the maintenance outside of the building – you just take care of the inside of your unit. The downside to that, which can be significant if you don't do your homework, is that if there is no reserve fund – which means that the condominium board does not have a large pool of money set aside for the major capital repairs such as the roof, the parking garage, the pool, etc. – then they will be coming to the individual owners with a huge cash call. If you don't have the money, they can actually take back your unit. In other words, your control over your condo is limited. Also, you have the added cost of a monthly condominium fee, which can be substantial. If you are buying a brand new condominium, keep in mind that the board may sweeten the deal by asking for low condominium fees for the first two years at say $150 or $200 a month, which would be very manageable. However, in the third year, if they jump up to $450 your cash flow disappears. So you must do your homework and definitely have a lawyer with some experience in condominiums to review all the contracts.

Whatever type of property you finally choose, make sure you are informed and fore-warned about all the pros and cons. Become a bit of an expert because the more focused and educated you are, the easier it is to find out what the true value of those properties is in that particular location. Even if you have to spend months just tracking property sales in the area you are interested in, when an opportunity does present itself you'll know it's a good deal and you can jump on it quickly.

Nuts and bolts of your first deal

Once you identify what kind of property you want and where, you will need – as already mentioned in a previous chapter – a good realtor. Not just any realtor either, but the one specializing in the type of property you are after. How do you know if your agent specializes in that particular property? Take a look at the listings, and the agent with the most condominium listings is obviously a good starting point if you want to buy a condominium.

An advantage of working with a good agent is that he may have deals that are not listed on the MLS yet, or he has his ear to the ground and knows all the good deals. Still, an agent doesn't have to be your only source of information. You can be surfing the MLS site (**www.realtor.ca**) yourself and looking for your own deals.

However, if you really want to take it up a notch, you don't want to be locked into just one way of getting deals; you want to have multiple ways at your disposal, and that's where marketing comes into play.

Speaking of marketing, networking is very important. In your case, real estate investor clubs may be a good resource. Now, you might be wondering, "Why should I go where every other investor goes looking for a deal?" Well, for a variety of reasons. Not every investor is interested in the same properties as you are. They may be more advanced than you are and dealing on a different level. For example, I may come across single-family homes that look like a decent deal to me, so I might put them under contract and then offer them to other people in my investing network. Why? Because I'm not interested in single-family homes anymore but I can still make a small profit by assigning a good deal to another investor. There are a lot of other investors out there who are growing as well. They started off with single-family dwellings but are now looking at the larger multi-units and they want to get rid of their single homes so they will sell them off to other investors. All this to say, find a real estate investors club in your area and go to the meetings. And by the way, these clubs are also good places to look for a mentor and recommendations for your power team.

Do-it-yourself

Networking is definitely worth exploring, but don't stop there. You can also actively market yourself and go looking for deals. We mentioned before that you don't actually need an agent or a realtor in order to do real estate investing, so one of the best places to start is with 'For sale by owners' properties, also known as FSBO or FIZBO. Let's define what this concept is and why people try to sell their properties by themselves without a realtor.

The number one reason is a fairly obvious one. These vendors want to save a buck by not paying the agent's commission. Consequently, a lot of properties are going to be over-priced because these individuals don't know how to value their properties correctly, but just as they can be over-priced, they can also be undervalued. Your advantage over the vendors is that you know the market and they most likely don't; you also know how to negotiate and most home owners probably don't. So do use that edge to score some good deals.

I come across a lot of people who mistakenly believe their property is worth a lot more than it really is. Just be polite, thank them nicely for their time, leave your name and phone number for when reality finally smacks them on the side of the head, and move onto the next deal. You may even want to consider making a low ball offer with the idea being that if they really need to sell their house and they have been unsuccessful after several months, then they may contact you again.

For example, you spot a house that you estimate to be worth $170,000. You knock on the door and the owners tell you that they will sell for $200,000. You offer them $150,000. Unless they are desperate for a quick sale, they will probably refuse your offer, at least initially. What they don't realize is that most serious purchasers will look at their property within the first four weeks of it being advertised and even if the price is adjusted lower after four weeks it will be difficult to sell. This is why it is imperative for sellers to list their house for a realistic price initially. After three or four months the seller may revisit your initial offer of $150,000.

In my own experience, virgin investors pay too much for their first property, so I always tell people not to purchase the first one they see. There is a general rule of thumb that you look at 100 deals, make an offer on five, and buy one. Even if these numbers are not set in stone, you should be looking at quite a few deals before you purchase your first property.

Where do you find FIZBOs? Local newspaper listings, the Internet (sites such as craigslist and kijiji), and even driving around the neighbourhood. This kind of reconnaissance mission is called 'farming,' which basically means you are looking for deals and opportunities. Sometimes you might even see a house that's not even advertised for sale. It's easy to identify rental properties, as they are usually the ones with the long grass and flags in the window, broken windowpanes, beer bottles in the front yard, etc

If you find a property like that and it looks like a good house with a bad tenant, that might be a potential deal.

Personally, I prefer that people call me rather than the other way around. Why? Because this means they are potentially motivated sellers, interested in making a deal. In effect, they are chasing you and you are comfortably installed in the driver's seat. When I first started out, I placed a lot of ads saying that an investor is looking for properties. I received many calls from folks wanting to sell. One important lesson I learned was to ask the caller if their property was currently listed with an agent. If it was, then the seller would need to cancel the listing agreement or I would have to wait until the agreement expired, or else use the agent. I have found this to be a great source of potential investment opportunities in the past.

A lot of people who read those kinds of ads may not even be looking for buyers, but they may be having a bad time with their tenants and figure that maybe they should answer the ad and see where it leads. So it's an ad that has to be running all the time, and it has to stand out so it catches their attention and makes them want to look at it. I leave those ads running in the free weekly newspaper because it goes to absolutely every home and it covers a huge area for a low cost. You may choose to run similar ads on craigslist, kijiji, or anywhere else you think provides good exposure.

This, in a nutshell, is all you need to get started and get your very first deal.

Notes & Thoughts!

Chapter 5

Money Maker or Money Sucker?

Or how to analyze your deal

So far, we have talked about how the real estate game really works, we have talked about the importance of a team, and we have talked about how to find your deal. Now let's say you have decided on an area of town to invest in and on the kind of property you want to be focusing on. You looked at a whole bunch of deals and one of them really pops out at you as potentially a really good one, but how do you really know if it's a winner? In this chapter you'll learn how to analyze a deal, or, more specifically, how to determine the quality of your investment opportunity. Simply put (as the title of this chapter suggests), is this property a money maker or a money sucker? Is it going to put money in your pocket or take money out of your pocket?

It's not an easy task to make number crunching sound exciting and I'm not sure how to do that. This is what you have to do: Figure out if this deal is as good as you are hoping it is or being told it is, and in order to do that you need to get a few basic numbers and see if they make sense.

But first, you must know the cold hard truth about sellers. They are liars. Now I don't mean this in a malicious way, because most sellers are good honest people. What I do mean, however, is that you won't be told the whole truth!

I say they are fibbers because the numbers they will give you initially are going to be incorrect. How will you know that? It is safest to make the assumption that all the figures the sellers give you are incorrect. However, don't let the fear of fake numbers stop you in your tracks.

How do you get over this hurdle? Just assume that the numbers – especially if they look really, really good – are not based on reality. Move forward with the idea in your head that there's something wrong with the figures, but it's worth looking into anyway.

Crunching the numbers

First, let's look at income and expenses. The income is going to be your rent and any other sources of revenue that the property can generate, such as parking. You may be able to rent parking to the tenant or someone else in the neighbourhood. If you own a rental property that has laundry facilities, that's a source of potential income as well. But again, for your first investment you are looking at a single family home, and most likely your only source of revenue here is going to be your rent.

What happens if the house you are looking at is currently owner occupied? If the person who lives there owns the house and is not paying rent, how do you know what the rental income is going to be?

You will have to do some market research. Very simply, just look in the newspaper and see what similar properties are renting for in that neighbourhood. This is something you should have been doing all along anyhow as part of your analysis of the neighbourhood to help determine the values of properties. You should also be looking to see how much the market rents are for two-bedroom and three-bedroom homes, bungalows, three stories, all different types of houses. Also be aware of what the rents include; for example, do they include utilities such as water and heat? Will the tenant be expected to shovel snow or do other handy work?

Those details will give you an idea of your income potential, but you also have to figure out what the expenses associated with the property are. You will have property taxes, insurance, heating, hydro, water/ sewer, financing costs, etc. The beauty of a single-family home is that you can pass a lot of those expenses directly onto a tenant. These additional charges that you can pass on may include heat, hydro, water, grass cutting, snow plowing etc.

There are, however, certain costs/ expenses which you can't pass on to a tenant. These will include your property taxes, house insurance, and debt service (mortgage payment).

Who is managing the property? Even if you are doing it, you need to pay yourself or you need to allow for that expense. Then you have advertising costs, maintenance costs, bookkeeping etc. A lot of these expenses you can absorb by doing the work yourself, but you still need to recognize that there is a cost involved in operating that house.

There is a general rule of thumb that your expenses should never exceed 50% of your income (preferably lower), so for example, if you receive $1000 a month in rental income, then your expenses should be less than $500, excluding your mortgage payment. Once you have paid your mortgage, any money left over is your profit and your cash flow. You need to have certain expectations as to what your projected cash flow will be for you, and these numbers will be different for everybody.

Be realistic about cash flow

Let's first explain what cash flow really is. First you take your gross income, all the income from the property, and then subtract all of the expenses you are paying for that property. The money left over is called the net operating income or NOI. From that, you take away the cost of financing, which is your debt service or your mortgage. Any money that's left over after that is your cash flow. Quite simple, really.

Before you purchase a property, you should define what you are hoping for as your minimum positive cash flow. You have to be realistic; if you are thinking that you are going to get $300 a month per door, you are probably going to be very disappointed. So what *can* you expect as far as positive cash flow at the end of the month, after all your expenses and your debt has been paid down?

I have a target of $75 per door per month as my profit. When I say 'per door', that would mean, if it's a single-family house, $75 for that unit. If I have a 10-unit building, then my goal is $750. I always aim higher; if I can get more, great, but that's my absolute minimum.

How can a novice investor get these income and expense numbers? They will be provided to you by the seller and/or the listing agent. However, as I've already warned you, they will be inaccurate or skewed. Sellers/agents will often give you *potential* rents as opposed to *actual* rents, and you are not going to make money on potential rents. They will also – if it's near the end of a calendar year – give you the actual expenses for that year, which are accurate, but be aware that those numbers aren't going to be the same moving forward into the next year, so you should probably adjust them accordingly. So yes, these figures are all going to be provided for you, but once you have the property under contract, that's when you have to do some research yourself and ask for verification of expenses, such as the tax certificate. You also want to see an insurance certificate or contact your own insurance agent to get a quote. And you are going to want to see the water and sewer bills, the gas bills, and the hydro bills to verify that all the numbers they have shown you are accurate. You should also be aware that some sellers are not even aware of all the related expenses they may have for their property. Perhaps they have been doing the repairs themselves and not allowing for a labour cost, or perhaps they have had advertising costs they forgot about. You need to include all related costs in order to determine the true value for the property.

Estimate your expenses

Let's say you know what the owners paid in expenses last year. How does that help you with this year's (as well as future) numbers?

It really depends on who's holding the portfolio. If it's a single-family residence owned by a home owner and the house is his principal residence, the insurance that he has paid last year is going to be less than the insurance you are going to pay when you turn the house into an investment property. Their insurance would be lower because it's home owner occupied, so you should anticipate an increase of maybe as high as 50%.

Then there are taxes. If it's a single family home and you are buying it for $200,000 but for whatever reason it was assessed at $100,000, the taxes are being calculated on the assessed value. When you purchase that house, the new assessed value is going to be closer to $200,000, so your taxes could almost double in one year. There are some communities, on the East Coast I think, where the assessment stays based upon the original purchase price, which means that somebody who bought a house 20 years ago for $50,000 is still paying taxes on it based on that price.

So when you, the investor, turn around and buy that property for $200,000, that's when you trigger a new assessment, so you must be aware of that. Since the process changes from region to region, the best thing to do is to contact the local tax office or your municipal authorities and find out what the tax rates and the mill rates are (the mill rate is a number that the municipality applies to the assessed value of the property to come up with the tax number). Once you know the mill rate and the taxes, you can figure the rest out. It's very simple.

Another big expense that's very rarely mentioned by sellers is maintenance. As a landlord, you are legally responsible to maintain your property. It doesn't mean you have to go in and clean the carpets or anything of that nature, but if something breaks, you are responsible to fix or replace it. If you are supplying the appliances and one of them breaks, you have to repair it, so that's something you may not want to provide. If you can cut maintenance costs or potential maintenance costs such as not supplying appliances, that's just smart management. These are things you can't get away from, so you've got to put a number in there to budget from.

Estimating future maintenance fees is not that easy because you basically have to estimate how many more years the furnace will last and how much a new furnace will cost. You need to know how much money you will need to be putting away towards the replacement cost of a new furnace to be installed at some time in the future or when it blows up.

There are annual maintenance fees and also what we call capital cost maintenance fees. All those big ticket items things like your furnace, roof, and hot water tank are your capital costs. When you are initially taking a look at a property to decide whether you want to buy it and you are going through your inspection, I would recommend that over and above all else, you have the furnace inspected by a furnace technician because if there's something wrong with it at that point, the seller would have to fix it before you buy the property. Alternatively, you may agree to do the repairs yourself, but negotiate a reduced sale price.

I've learned this the hard way – it would have cost me $75 to have a furnace technician check the furnace. It cost me $5,000 the day after I owned the property to find out it was defective and subsequently red tagged, meaning that it could not be used, effective immediately. So you need to know that stuff ahead of time because that's a huge hit to your pocket when you've got to spend $5,000 unexpectedly within the first week of ownership in the middle of winter.

Of course, there are no guarantees. Say the furnace is eight years old and it's got a life expectancy of 15 years, and your hot water tank is three years old and it should last another seven to 10 years. You calculate all of these numbers and if you know that you are going to need about $10,000 in five years to repair the roof, the tank and the furnace, you'd better start saving money on an annual basis, so at the end of five years of putting away $2000 a year, you have $10,000. Or you can gamble a little bit and budget that capital cost into the future refinancing. In five years time, you know the mortgage on the property will be paid down by approximately 4% per year (very rough estimate) and the value will have increased by a certain percentage due to appreciation, so you refinance the house, take some equity out and use it for capital repairs. So basically there are two ways of looking at it.

Again, find out all of those expenses, figure out how much they are going to be for the year, and that's what you are looking for when crunching numbers. Additionally, when you purchase a property, you are going to add some one-time hard costs that you need to take into consideration upfront. This will affect the amount of money you need to bring to the lawyer's office at closing in order to buy this property. These can include an appraisal, but it depends on where you are getting the financing. How much are the legal fees? These are questions you can ask your lawyer ahead of time, since he can give you a ballpark figure of how much it's going to cost to do a transaction. And what about the home inspection? In fact, you might want to budget for two home inspections just in case you have to get a roofer to come in as well. Other expenses depend on the area – in British Columbia and Ontario, for example, you'll have land transfer tax, and in Toronto there are two land transfer tax charges. So these are some of the highest hard costs you need to be aware of ahead of time. Your lawyer will help identify these costs so that you shouldn't have any surprises.

Vacancy rate

Once you calculate your NOI as described above, you should allow for a vacancy rate because the property is not going to be 100% occupied all of the time. You can go on the Canada Housing and Mortgage Corporation (**http://www.cmhc-schl.gc.ca**) web site and find out what the vacancy rate is for your neighbourhood. Apply that number to your gross operating income, which will give you what is called the effective gross operating income which is the money that you should count on operating with. If you have no vacancies, that's a definite bonus, but count on having some vacancies because when you go to the bank for financing, they are going to base their calculations with a vacancy rate included.

Many sellers will tell you they never had a vacancy. That may well be the case, but what happens if you buy the property and within the first month the tenant moves out and says that she/he told the previous owner they were moving? Then you have a vacant house, but if you have budgeted for this then you should be okay. That's a scenario you should never overlook.

Then there are other vacancy-related costs you should take into account, such as marketing. If you have an empty unit not generating any income, you will want to spend a few bucks to get a new tenant in there. You don't have to budget thousands of dollars; even a couple of hundred will go a long way to cover the advertising costs. Thankfully, there are a lot of places where you can advertise for free, like the internet and local community bulletin boards, at laundromats, grocery stores, etc. The most cost effective and productive advertising method will be a sign on your property or in the front window. You'll probably get 40%-50% response on that sign, but I suggest you take it one step further and go to a local sign maker shop, have a nice one made, and put it out on the front lawn so that it looks professional. You can probably get a nice sign for about $50 or $60. This will look much better than the signs you buy at the local hardware store and it will help differentiate you from other landlords.

You may be wondering by now about other vacancy-generated costs such as cleaning the place up after a tenant leaves. That basically falls under your maintenance, but it is definitely not to be overlooked and the great value of that comes more under the management chapter.

We are not quite done yet…

We talked about a lot of expenses you should budget in, but there is one more consideration to help determine the true value – comparables. The value of an income generating property is determined primarily by the cash flow it generates but single family home values are generally determined by comparables.

Basically, you should find out what the property you are looking at is actually worth. The way to determine that is to look at recent comparables with the other homes, similar in style, age, and condition, in the area that have sold within the past six months. If they all sold for around $200,000 and you're paying $250,000, then maybe you are overpaying. Again, that is going to be determined once you research that particular neighbourhood for a period of time. If you don't understand how to do this, get your realtor to pull some comparables for you.

This is where a realtor can be really valuable to you because he/she has access to the behind-the-scenes numbers. He/she can go back a few years and see how much a property has sold for in that time. It takes them minutes to pull up five comparables in your neighbourhood of properties that have sold in the past six months just to confirm that the price you are paying is reasonable.

Another thing you want to know is the appreciation for your area. Is this an area that's flat and not going up, going up only 1-2%, or is it located in a neighbourhood next door to a 'yuppieville', so you can expect your area to take off as well? It may be flat today, but tomorrow it might go up 5% or 8%, or even 10%. You obviously want to be investing in an up and coming neighbourhood if you can. Try to find out what the future development plans are for the neighbourhood and if there is good mass transit close by or if there are plans to extend the public transit closer to your location. Is there any new industry coming to town, are there any planned business closures, is the local municipal government marketing the area for growth? These types of questions will help determine what the potential future holds for the neighbourhood. If possible, you certainly would prefer to invest in a market that has potential growth.

Another thing you want to look at is finances, or in other words, how much is your money going to cost, not only on loan value, but also how much are you going to ask from the bank or broker to finance this particular property? Obviously, the less money you put down, the lower your cash flow and the higher your expenses will be, because you are paying more money to the bank. On the other hand, the more you get from the bank, the less of your own cash you have to put in.

This is to say you need to weigh the pros and cons here. If you have unlimited cash to put into the deal, what will be the effect of getting 60% financing from the bank and you coming up with the balance, versus getting 90% from the bank and you only coming up with 10%? Obviously, your cash flow is going to go down but maybe that's okay because you can buy four properties instead of just one.

Do talk to your mortgage broker and ask him/her to explain the pros and cons of the different terms and rates that are available to you, and what would work best for you. If this is a property you are planning to hang onto, then you may want to consider locking in and having a fixed interest rate. If you're thinking of just buying it for a year or two, you might want to go with a variable rate.

At the end of the day, you have to see if the property meets your goals and requirements. Is it in the location you are looking for, the kind of house you want to buy, and does it meet your minimum criteria for cash flow and the other things that you are looking for in terms of built-in equity, cash flow, leverage, all the six different profit centres that we looked at? You must keep a cool head about this and not get emotionally attached to the property because it is just an income generator, not the object of your affection.

Although you may hate crunching numbers, all of the above points are crucial to master if you want to end up with a profitable real estate investment.

I have included a picture of a very simple to use, yet effective property analyzer which I use when I determine the viability of a property. Using an analyzer of this nature will help you identify many expenses you might otherwise over look. It also provides you with targets located in the 'Key Indicator' box which are just that, targets. For example, you will see I have a target of $50,000 cost per door which is virtually impossible to achieve for a single family home. This target is set for larger multi-unit properties so when I'm looking at a single home or even a duplex, I would ignore this target.

One of the benefits of a good analyzer is that it will prevent you from overlooking any of the obvious expenses and some of the less obvious expenses. It can help calculate the potential cash flow with financing in place and it can easily show you different cash flow scenarios when you change some of your expenses and financing values.

INSTRUCTIONS

Property Info	
Address	n/a
Number of Doors	0
Local Cap Rate	7.0%
Local Appreciation	3.0%
Asking Price	0
Market Value	0
Purchase Price (PP)	0

Purchase Costs		
Appraisal		0
Legal Fees		0
Inspection		0
Land Transfer Tax		0
Repairs / Improvements	+	0
Total Purchase Costs		0
Seller Rebate	-	0
Purchase Costs After Rebate		**0**

Cash Requirements		
Down Payment		0
Purchase Costs	+	0
LESS: Cash Back	-	0
Total Cash Required		**0**

<< NOTES >>

Income		Annual
Rent		0
Parking		0
Laundry		0
Other	+	0
Gross Operating Income (GOI)		0
Vacancy Rate	(5%) -	0
Effective GOI		**0**

Expenses		Annual
Property Taxes		0
Insurance		0
Water / Sewer		0
Heat (Gas)		0
Hydro (Electicity)		0
Maintenance	(800/dr)	0
Management	(8%)	0
Snow Removal		0
Super Intendant		0
Advertising		0
Supplies		0
Garbage		0
Lawn		0
Licenses		0
Accounting		0
Legal		0
Cleaning		0
Pool		0
Elevator		0
Pest Control		0
Replacements		0
Condo Fees		0
Other	+	0
Total Expenses		**0**

Financing	Mort #1	Mort #2	Mort #3
% of Purchase Price	85.0%	0.0%	0.0%
Loan Amount	0	0	0
Loan to Value (LTV)	n/a	n/a	n/a
Payment Type	Pri+Int	Pri+Int	Pri+Int
Amortization	35 yrs	35 yrs	0 yrs
Interest Rate	6.00%	6.00%	6.00%
Montly Interest Rate	0.49%	0.49%	0.49%
Apply for Mortgage Insurance?	Yes	No	No
Mortgage Premium	0.40%	0.00%	0.00%
CMHC Fee	0	0	0
Year 1 Principal Paydown (PPD)	0	0	0
Monthly Payment	**0**	**0**	**0**

Cashflow Summary	Monthly	Annual
Net Operating Income (NOI)	0	0
Annual Debt Service (ADS) -	0	0
Total Cashflow (CF)	**0**	**0**

Key Indicators	Actual	Target
Cost Per Door	n/a	< 50,000
Gross Rent Multiplier (GRM)	n/a	< 7
Cap Rate	n/a	> 9%
Cash on Cash Return (ROI)	n/a	
ROI + PPD	n/a	
ROI + PPD + 3% Growth	n/a	> 50%
Avg. Monthly Profit / Door	n/a	> 75
Debt Coverage Ratio	n/a	> 1.2
Payback Period	n/a	< 1 yr

Potential Taxable Income		Annual
Est. Projected Cash Flow		0
Yr1 Principle Pay Down	+	0
Depreciation	-	0
Mortgage Ins. expense	-	0
Potential Taxable Income		**0**

There are many analyzers available out there, so I would suggest you use one that is recommended to you by another successful investor, keeping in mind that it should not be a complicated analyzer or else you could easily become overwhelmed. Live by the KISS principle (keep it simple, stupid).

I highly recommend using a property analyzer in order to help determine if the property will be a Money Maker or a Money Sucker, but you must remember that it is just a tool. It can be a very useful tool, but you need to learn and understand what to look for, what questions to ask, and how to determine the true cash flow.

Having a seasoned real estate agent who has also invested in rental properties will be a great asset to you during this process. This is why it is so important to have properly qualified team members helping you. Do not let the fear of making a mistake stop you at this point like it does so many others. You will make mistakes. We all do. This is why you start small with a single-family investment property. Any mistakes made at this level of investing are manageable and easier to overcome than if you buy a 12-unit building. Learn from your mistakes like I have, and you will become a better investor.

To see it in use, and to get a copy of Ken Beaton's Real Estate Analyzer for yourself, visit **www.RealEstateFirstTimers.com**

Notes & Thoughts!

CHAPTER 6

HOW TO MAKE AN OFFER – AND GET THE HOUSE!

Up to now we talked about how the real estate game really works, we got our team together, we figured out how to find a deal, and we also learned how to crunch numbers. Now we will look at how to make an offer on the property you want to buy.

The first thing after analyzing the property is determining what is the highest price you are prepared to pay, and then sticking to it. That's not the offer price you are going to make because – unlike going to a store and just buying a piece of clothing off the rack for the quoted price – we don't do that in real estate. Basically, you go in with a low offer and be open to negotiations.

When I was just starting out, I was very uncomfortable negotiating because I am the type of person who pays the asking price. But that rule doesn't apply to real estate. Here's the challenge: You have to be careful not to go in too low and insult the seller to the point that they don't want to deal with you anymore. The offer has to be realistic but also lower than what you are prepared to pay. So set those parameters to begin with. Then you have to actually draft up a purchase and sale agreement, which can be as simple as a piece of paper. I would strongly recommend, however, that for your first deal you get a real estate agent to draft the paperwork because the process changes from province to province; if you are buying something in, say, British Columbia, it could be different than if you are purchasing in Prince Edward Island.

Getting an agent can make all the difference

Say you found a property yourself, negotiated the terms, and want to buy it directly from the owner. You have been acting solo, but now you have to translate all that information into a document to make it legal and binding. This is where you'd be smart to bring in a real estate agent, even though the agent is not going to be paid by the seller. There are a couple of ways to do that. One of them is called a seller's or a buyer's commission.

When an agent is hired by somebody to sell a house, he is paid a commission by the seller, but in this case you will pay the commission, so you might want to set up a contract for a set amount or a percentage. If you opt for the latter, the percentage would typically be around 3%-4% of the purchase price, though it could be as low as 2%.

However, you'd probably be better off opting for a flat fee, let's say $1000 or $1500 for the whole service instead of the percentage, because the agent is not really doing that much, just the paperwork.

Once you bring in a professional to help you with the paperwork, he will walk you through the whole process, mostly a lot of legal numbers, addresses, and things like that. He will also explain to you what's included in the sale, and what isn't. For example, included are standard fixtures such as the hot water tank, furnace, and central air, but you could ask for the appliances as well.

But generally the agent will tell you what's commonly included and what isn't.

Here's an important point to make whether you are buying your first property or your hundredth: When you decide on a property to purchase, it is highly recommended that you document what you are asking for. For instance, if you are asking for the stainless steel fridge and stove in the kitchen, you'd better specify that you want the stainless steel fridge and stove along with model numbers XXXX to remain in that kitchen or else you might end up with the old bar fridge from the basement and a used stove, while the owners take the upgraded appliances with them when they move. Another great way to circumvent this is to take pictures of everything in the house. While you are doing the viewing, ask for permission to take some pictures just for your own personal reference, so the house's contents can't be disputed later. If somebody tries to pull a quick one on you and replace the appliances, when you take the property over you can go in with the photos and say this is what I bought.

Escape clauses to protect yourself

When you are making an offer, you are not buying the property yet, all you are doing is creating what we call an option to buy through a purchase and sale agreement. Part of the option is that the sale is conditional on meeting various criteria. One of the criteria is financing. For example, you insert a clause saying something to the effect of, "This deal is conditional upon us obtaining financing satisfactory to ourselves. If we are unable to obtain that financing, this deal shall be dead."

This is a smart move because you don't know if you'll be able to get the money for that particular property, since it's not only you who have to qualify, but also the house.

In other words, you want to make sure that you have an escape door in this deal so you aren't bound to it if you change your mind later or are unable to obtain the funds to purchase. Not only that, but as mentioned in a previous chapter, you have to go under the assumption that a lot of numbers provided to you by the seller are incorrect, so the bank may turn you down or you might decide that you want to renegotiate because the end deal doesn't look anywhere as good as the initial one.

Another escape clause or 'subject to' clause will relate to inspection(s). I put (s) because it's not just one inspection; you want to have the option or the ability to have multiple inspections. This will allow your home inspector and furnace inspector to check the property and make sure it's in as good a condition as described by the seller. If you discover a problem that needs to be rectified, then you can renegotiate the deal or you can walk away; you have that option.

Here's another clause to include: "Conditional upon the seller providing the buyer with one year's worth of property tax bills, water bills, hydro bills, heating bills etc." If you are buying a single-family home that's already used as a rental property, or even if it is a single-family home that's owner occupied, you need to verify what the property taxes are – the hydro, the heat expense, the water expense, all the expenses that are related to that property. Remember, the seller may not be giving you correct numbers, so get the documents and actual receipts for what the current owners paid for taxes, insurance, utilities, etc.

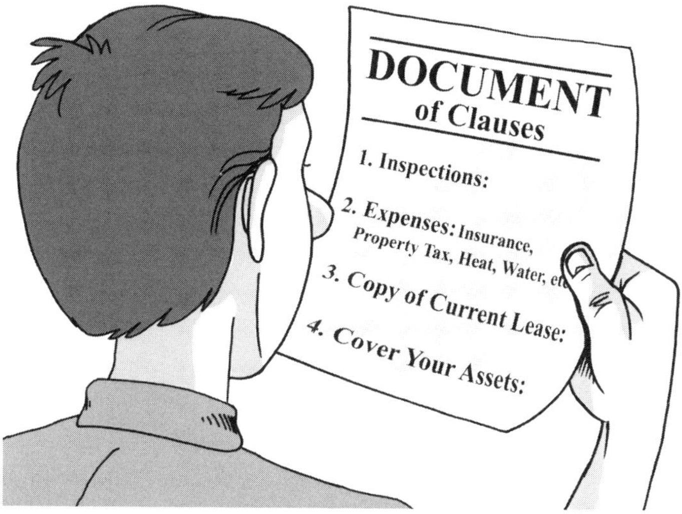

This would also be the time to contact your insurance agent and verify what they are going to charge you, and also calculate what the property taxes are going to be after you buy the property.

The next clause, if this is a rental property, is to get a copy of the lease of the current tenant. Verify that the rent is what the seller says it is, and also that it's a legal rent; that it hasn't been artificially inflated; that it is paid every month and there are no arrears; and that the tenant is happy and going to be there for another six months or a year, whatever the case may be. Ideally you are trying to determine if the current tenant is a good tenant who pays their rent on time, and is in good standing. Try to get a statement of their payment history, although likely most landlords won't have this level of detail.

The last clause that you really need to include in your document is one called the CYA clause, which basically means 'Cover Your Assets'. This clause will typically say something like, "Conditional for X days, subject to my lawyer's approval." For this and other clauses it's imperative that you contact a real estate attorney who, as previously mentioned, should be a member of your power team. He or she will look at the deal objectively to protect your interests, and if for whatever reason you get cold feet at this point and just decide you want out, this is the best escape clause for you. But assuming you want to move forward, your lawyer is going to tell you where any possible glitches are or, if everything looks good, will give you the green light.

By the way, the CYA clause will only be in your document for a few days after the contract has been created. It's like a cooling off period for the buyer to think hard about whether he is going to go through with the sale, but it's also an opportunity for the lawyer to look at the deal and confirm that structurally it looks fine. The lawyer is not looking at the history of the property yet; that comes two to three weeks before closing.

Clauses in place, what's next?

All these clauses are usually added into what is called a 'Schedule A', and attached to the main purchase and sale agreement. In the body of the actual Purchase and Sale agreement, you have legal information about the buyer, the seller, and the property itself – what's included, what's excluded, we've gone through that. But there is also an important date, called the 'irrevocability date'. The first time you create this document, you are going to put a date somewhere in there – and that's where your agent is going to help you. Basically, you are telling the seller, "I am going to give you X number of days to think about this offer. If I don't hear back from you before this time frame, then this offer is null and void." If they accept the offer, that's the end of the negotiations. If they don't like the terms, any terms, and they make a change to that document, technically the deal is dead until you accept those changes. They are going to change that irrevocability date – another word for 'deadline' – if there's not enough time for you to think about it. So that's how it goes back and forth; it can be done in as little as an hour or it can take a month, which is extreme.

'Irrevocability date', by the way, is not to be confused with a completion date, which states when the deal is going to close, and there will be change of ownership from the seller to you. That obviously needs to be clearly defined and set out, and it has to be far enough away from your negotiations to give your lawyer enough time to do his research.

By the way, you might be wondering what's a good rule of thumb for a first-time buyer in getting organized with the financing. I would strongly suggest you speak with a mortgage broker prior to making any offers in order to become prequalified for financing. You will still need to make the offer conditional upon financing because the property itself will also need to qualify for financing. For a single family home this time frame could be as little as two days but I would suggest you ask for two weeks which is not unreasonable.

Now, let's say your completion date is two months ahead, and your conditional clause(s) is/are usually a week to two weeks down the road. After you get a deal put together, you have a week to two weeks to get your financing in place, do your inspections, etc., and then you still have another six weeks to close. Your lawyer will use this time period to do a title search on the property to insure that everything is in order with the title of the property.

Another very important point that a lot of people overlook is the confirmation of execution. Again, that can be called different things in different provinces, but quite simply, the confirmation of execution happens upon the completion of negotiations between the buyer and the seller. Once both sides have agreed to all of the information in the initial purchase and sale agreement, the last person to make the changes, initial, and sign the agreement has to sign a confirmation of execution box, which is basically like the starter pistol being fired for all of your conditions to begin. The time clock starts ticking at that point. For example, if you begin the negotiations on Friday and the negotiations continue back and forth over the weekend, then Monday at noon you reach a mutual agreement, that is the day that the timeline starts for your conditions to be fulfilled.

For instance, say you have two weeks for the financing, so you negotiate back and forth. Two weeks from that Monday is when the timeline expires for your financing; if you haven't got it by then, you either need to ask for an extension of conditions or lose the deal.

What happens if part of the negotiation is that you want something fixed? In this case, you are going to create a condition that can be fulfilled at any time; if it's not, the deal doesn't close or it gets postponed, or else there's a penalty attached to it. There are different ways to structure that. This is where it can get complicated and you definitely need to work with a lawyer.

Let's say that during the inspection of the property you discover that the shingles on the garage should be replaced and the estimated cost will be $3,000. The seller agrees to change the shingles prior to the closing date and if the seller has not done so then he/she agree to pay to the purchaser $3,000. This is good for you as the purchaser because you don't have to come up with the money after closing in order to do the required work.

Important considerations for closing the deal

Let's say you and the seller have agreed to a deal; now what? To make this a legally binding contract in Canada, money has to change hands. But no agent will allow you to pay or accept a toonie as a consideration, so the seller is going to insist that you put down a deposit as a sign of good faith and a lot of agents will try to convince you to put down a significant amount.

How much? For a single-family home of $200,000, they'd probably try to get $5000 down, but for me personally that's ridiculous. For a house like that, I would put down a $500 deposit. If they really balk at it, then I would say, "Fine, here's $500 down now, once I waive all my conditions, in other words when I am satisfied with my financing, my inspection and due diligence, I will give you another $4500." I don't mind adding more to the deposit at that point in time, because I know for certain that I am going to purchase the house. Of course, be prepared to be pressured to put down more than $500, but just keep in mind that you don't have to.

Now, as I already mentioned, the best way to negotiate is to get an opportunity to speak with the vendors directly, to understand what they want. If you can satisfy those expectations, then you can have a much easier time putting a deal together. The best deals I have ever experienced were deals where I could speak directly with the seller so that I could develop a relationship. It's extremely valuable to get as much information as possible about what's motivating the vendors to sell that property so that you may create a win-win scenario.

Basically, you are trying to make it a win-win deal, without anybody being taken advantage of. I mentioned earlier that you should not go in with a low-ball offer, but less than what you are actually willing to pay. Don't go in with your bottom line offer without any negotiation, because there's no wiggle room there.

An example may be that the house is selling for $200,000, but you know the sellers aren't really expecting to get that sum. You are hoping to buy it for $190,000, that's your ceiling. So you might go in at $180,000; they'll counter back at $195,000, you'll counter back at $185,000, and magically you'll end up at $190,000. This way the sellers won't feel like they have been taken advantage of.

Speaking of prices, I mentioned earlier that you don't want to reveal your upper limit number to your real estate agent; you want to keep that information close to your chest. If the listing agent knows what you are willing to pay then they will inform the seller of this which will then make it much more difficult for you to negotiate. Only divulge what information is truly necessary and no more, but always ask questions like, "How much do you feel the house will sell for?" The agents are not allowed to divulge such information to you, but many agents will talk openly about what they feel the property will sell for.

Negotiating well is truly an art, but for the first time try to keep it simple – rely on the numbers, and if the numbers make sense, don't worry too much about the price.

Remember that this is your first deal so you are naturally excited, but if you are not careful, if you are going to be guided by emotion, you won't do well. Get that out of your mind, and always remember that you are willing to walk away from the deal if it doesn't make sense to you.

Be informed, stay as cool as a cucumber, be aware of potential pitfalls, and ask professional advice when needed.

Notes & Thoughts!

CHAPTER 7

CLOSING THE DEAL

The seller has accepted your offer and you included some clauses in the contract to make sure your interests are protected. What do you do before money actually changes hands?

Your offer to purchase is simply that – an *option*. Remember that you can still change your mind. If you look at the purchase and sale agreement, you will see that the Schedule A has ‘subject to clauses’ or ‘conditional clauses’ with timelines. As those timelines expire, you have to decide with each condition if you are going to waive and accept it, or whether you are going to walk away from the deal because – in case you have any doubts or second thoughts later – you can no longer change your mind on that condition. If the financing has been approved and you accept it and waive that condition, you can’t go back later and say you changed your mind.

Therefore, you must make sure that you have completed all your due diligence during those time frames, due diligence being your homework. And, as mentioned several times before, do work with a lawyer who not only knows real estate, but also is familiar with the laws and regulations of that particular province.

Before you waive your last condition, take a look at the numbers once more because now you have the accurate figures and you understand the property better. Analyze the numbers again with a keen eye to detail; if it all still makes sense and you want to move forward, then you will waive that last condition. Again, if there are any glitches that have been discovered during your due diligence, such as a repair that wasn't discussed in the initial purchase and sale agreement, now is the time to negotiate to have this repair paid for because once you waive that final condition, your leverage is gone.

Basically, this is your last opportunity to really dig in and make sure that you know what the real numbers are, what the real condition of the property is, and see if it all still makes sense to you. If it doesn't, this is a chance to renegotiate, reopen the deal and try to make it work for you. Let's say, for example, that you find out the furnace will have to be replaced within the next six months to a year. It is going to cost $5000, not to mention the pain in the butt factor which can't be measured in monetary terms, but it's still something to consider.

It is up to you to decide what you are willing to accept as compensation. Maybe you are open to splitting the cost with the vendor and reducing the price by $2500, or perhaps the seller agrees to replace the furnace before closing with a model of your choosing, in which case you can include it in the financing. You don't adjust the price but you get a new furnace. If the seller says, "Too bad, take it or leave it," then you have to decide whether spending $5000 more than you had intended will be worth it? These are the factors you have to look at and consider at this time.

So you have to crunch numbers again, look at your new insurance cost and taxes, and compare that with the amount of rent being paid. This is where you see if it still makes sense for your cash flow. If it doesn't, go back to the seller and say, "Look, here's the bottom line. I need to be making at least $50 a month off this house for it to make any sense. However, the numbers show it won't work that way. What can we do to make it work?" That's an excellent tactic that I use all the time. I sit down with the sellers, bring out my analyzer, and show them the numbers. I talk to them in a non-condescending, respectful way, explaining that this is a business to me and if doesn't make business sense, what's the point of buying that property? When the sellers realize that you have all the numbers worked out and you know what you are talking about, they are likely to be more willing to lower their expectations and be flexible on the price.

I don't want to sound like a broken record, but this point bears repeating: Never forget that you are purchasing this property as an investment. It's not about emotions; it's all about cold hard numbers that have to make business sense to you. And if the sellers won't cooperate with you, remember that there are many more deals out there.

Other things to take care of before the closing

Here's something else to keep in mind: If anything is discovered to be out of order, broken, or not functioning properly prior to closing, then your lawyer will talk to the seller's lawyer, they'll negotiate back and forth, and get it all cleaned up. If, for whatever reason, the deficiency can't be taken care of, then the deal is not going to close at that point. If that were to happen, you wouldn't be held liable for not closing, providing it is the seller's fault. If you suddenly get cold feet and don't want to close the deal, then you will be held liable and forced to close the deal.

On the day of the closing, when you actually receive the keys to the property, you have to show up at the lawyer's office with your money order or cash, and pay for the closing costs as well as the difference between the financing and the purchase price. All of the legal stuff is taken care of on that particular day and you technically own the property. My advice is to try to close after the first week of the month. Why? Because if it is a rental property, you are allowing the seller to collect the rent for that month. The seller will collect the rent and the lawyer will then adjust the amount you owe the seller at closing so there's that much less money you have to bring to the table. Even more importantly, you don't have to knock on the tenant's door asking for rent on the day you close the deal. It gives you some time to build a relationship with your tenant, and the owner of the property has to pay the rent to you for that month.

One more thing, send a really nice letter to your tenant introducing yourself and letting them know what your expectations are. Try to develop a cordial relationship from day one. This is where the aforementioned 'people skills' come in handy.

Congratulations, you own an investment property!

This is what you wanted all along, but now that your signature is there, black on white, you are scared! Some new purchasers even feel terrified. After all, you just committed lots of money, either your own or other people's, so you now must make this investment work. How do you deal psychologically with this new responsibility?

You may think the scariest moment is the actual signing of the purchase and sale agreement. You are sitting in the lawyer's office and are overwhelmed with the amount of paperwork that he is placing in front of you – at least four copies of everything, including all those guarantees that you have to sign. That's the way banks operate; they want more guarantees than anybody else in the world, but all the investors have to go through this, so it's standard. And if your lawyer approved the terms, then you should not be overly nervous. There is always a shot of whiskey if you need it!

Still, a bit of nervousness for a first-time investor is not unusual or unreasonable. It's a very sobering moment, to say the least, when you realize that you are now responsible for another property that is a home to your tenant. In a way, the first property is like the first-born child – you are fretting about it, not sure whether you can live up to all the responsibilities. You can and you will.

With time, as you purchase more properties, things will get easier. You will see this house as a way of creating wealth for yourself and your family. Try to keep that big picture in mind when you are getting nervous jitters at the closing table – don't sweat it, it's all good. You've done your homework, you feel confident with it, and you've crunched your numbers. If the deal makes sense and the numbers make sense, have confidence in your decision and be excited about it.

Go out and celebrate. But not too much; now that you are a real estate investor, you have to keep a cool head!

Notes & Thoughts!

Chapter 8

Managing the Property – It's Not Always Smooth Sailing

You closed the deal, bought the property, and celebrated. Now what?

As mentioned at the end of the previous chapter, a good way to get started with your new tenant – assuming there's already one in the place – is to send a little letter of introduction outlining what your expectations are, and start building a relationship.

Establishing a good relationship with your tenant is important. Here's why: What we often refer to as property management is easy. The real work comes in managing people, so it's fair to say that people management is equally as important as the property management itself, yet it's all grouped together. What I would like to do is break it apart and categorize it under 'property management' and 'people management'. Let's start with property management.

When I am talking about property management, I mean managing the physical property itself, the operations of the property. Even if you hire property management services in the future, try to manage the property and pay the bills yourself for at least six months to a year to get a handle on what is involved. That way when you do hire a property manager, you will have a clearer idea of what to expect of them.

Keeping an eye on your operations, even if someone else is managing them for you, is crucial to maintain control and make sure everything is going as it should. Some good friends of mine almost went bankrupt as a result of improper management and not overseeing how the money was spent on their property. So if you don't pay all the expenses yourself, make sure that whoever does, makes the payments on time.

If you have a new tenant moving in, be proactive about that as well. Go to the property yourself and make sure the unit is in an excellent move-in condition. You don't want a tenant to move into the property and find leaking taps. Not only will leaking taps cost you money in water bills, it may also send a negative message to the new tenant that you don't care, but if the place is in good shape and everything works as it should, you will attract and keep better tenants. That is going to save you money in the long run, because better tenants will not only cause less damage to the property, but they will also take good care of it, maybe even doing some repairs and maintenance work at their own expense.

When you have a new tenant moving in, do a complete inspection of the property, especially if someone else had been living there previously. Again, be proactive and repair all of the deficiencies you may discover, and then do an inspection with your new tenant to make sure he is happy with the condition. Document everything, so if there's ever a problem down the road, you have proof that the damage was created by the tenant and was not there originally. On the other hand, if you lack that documentation, you don't have any legal grounds to stand on which will make it very difficult if you need to prove the tenant caused the damage.

It is a good idea to inspect your property annually or, better yet, twice a year. Look for leaky taps, leaky toilets, doors and windows not closing properly. If you do find anything that has to be repaired, have it fixed within a week. Again, it's very impressive to the tenant, and good for you to maintain and extend the life of the property.

What about damage inflicted by the tenant, say holes in the wall or cigarette burns in the carpet? In cases like these, you can give them the option of doing the repairs themselves or have you do the repairs and bill them. But again, if you don't have that initial, documented inspection, you will have no grounds to go after them for the cost.

Things every landlord must know

Another thing you, as a landlord, must do is your smoke detector inspection. If you do not have a smoke detector inspection at least once a year, then you aren't protecting your assets because if there's a fire, and if there's a life lost as a result of that fire, you can be held legally liable if you can't prove that there was a working smoke detector in the unit. You are going to be fined and/or serve time in jail, so that could potentially be a very serious situation for all involved. But if you have the smoke detector inspected and tested at least once a year (changing the battery if necessary), and the tenant signs off on it, you are protected. I would suggest you do this inspection at least twice a year which can be tied in with the Fall and Spring time change. This will provide a total of four inspections per year which will help deter any potential illegal activities from taking place as well.

While you are at it, make sure you have a smoke detector on every floor, including the basement. The best thing is to check with your local fire department to find out what the regulations are for your area, and make sure you are fully compliant.

Vetting tenants

If you think managing your physical property is your biggest challenge, think again. Actually, managing the property is the easiest part; dealing with clients can be a joy or a nightmare.

Never forget that you are running a business, not a social club. While you should be courteous and respectful toward your tenants, do not befriend them. If you do, they may treat you like a friend too, and maybe not pay their rent on time and expect you to overlook it, or not maintain the property and think you might turn a blind eye. In other words, mixing business with pleasure is not in your best interest.

Now, before you actually rent your unit, you need to learn how to screen and qualify tenants. As a new landlord, you'd be wise to seek out the network and the power of real estate or landlord clubs for advice; even if it means you have to drive some distance to meetings, it is a valuable resource and you can learn from other people's mistakes.

Okay, back to the tenant. You should create a screening questionnaire so when you are talking to a prospective tenant on the phone, you can ask them pertinent questions during the course of the conversation. The answers to these questions will help you decide whether you are interested in renting to this particular person or not. You have to be extremely careful and aware of what you can or cannot ask – here the landlord or real estate club will be helpful to you again. If and when you decide that these clients are of interest, then you can send them an application asking for personal information, as well as permission to pull a credit check.

How do you go about doing a credit check? There are several ways. I subscribe to a service called 'Rent Check'. Once you become a landlord, you can join this service for a very reasonable annual fee. You can then send your client's information on to them and they will pull the credit check for you.

Or you can send the application to your mortgage broker asking him to run a credit check providing they are willing to do so. However, to be able to do that, you must ask the client's permission to share the information included in the application with a third party such as your mortgage broker. To that end, have your lawyer create the application, and if you are going to rely on the broker to help with the credit checks, ask him to take a look as well, to make sure all the correct information is included. You might want to tell the potential clients that the credit check is primarily being used to determine that they have been consistent with their debt payments. Here too, rules vary among provinces, so you need to understand what yours are.

If you don't want to ask your lawyer to devise an application form, both Google and real estate or landlord clubs are good resources of this information. But again, if you do seek out legal advice, be aware that there are attorneys who specialize in tenant-landlord relationships, and they are the ones you'd want to see.

When it comes time to create a lease, each province is going to be a little bit different. Whatever the provincial lease says you have to provide, you have to provide. You can't add something else to the lease that's going to change the effect of whatever is in the initial lease. However, you can add your own rules and regulations to it.

Now, let's assume your tenant has or wants to have a pet. Or he wants to rent your garage. Should you charge an extra fee?

It's up to you, but if you do want the tenant to pay additional fee for those 'extras', lay that all out in a Schedule A, an addendum to it. And let your lawyer review it, because you want to make sure that in the event of a conflict with your tenant, you have a solid legal ground to stand on as well as making sure it is legal to do so in your province.

When reviewing an application from a potential tenant, or when interviewing a candidate, be thorough and vigilant. Assume – just as you did when dealing with the seller during the negotiation process – that the tenant is fibbing. Therefore, you want to verify all the information given to you. For example, if the candidate claims he is making $15 an hour with ABC Construction Company and gives you the phone number and the contact person, follow up. And here's a little trick you can use. You might say, "Hi, I heard Joe Blow has been working for you for five years (when in fact the prospective tenant told you he had been working there for 10 years), and he's making $15 an hour." If it's his buddy posing as the reference, he will rack his brain for the correct answer. But if the person corrects you and tells you Joe Blow has actually been with the company for 10 years, chances are it's a legitimate reference. If, on the other hand, he says, "Oh yeah, that's about right," then you know it's a set-up. As you can see, there are little ways of tricking the references to see whether they are telling you the truth or not.

Any way you look at it, it is to your advantage to follow-up on references. You can judge people by appearances, by how they speak, whom they hang out with, etc. So the more access you can get to this type of information, the more accurate picture you will get of this person. For instance, when they show up to view the apartment, take a look at what they are driving. If they show up in a beat-up, dirty car filled with McDonalds bags and other trash, you can bet they will treat your property the same way.

One question to ask yourself is would I hire this individual if I were an employer? If the answer is "no", then you may not want to rent to him either.

Generally speaking (it's based on experience, not on science), out of 100 tenants out there, 10% are going to be horrendous, 10% are going to be your ideal tenants where you will never hear anything from them, and then 80% are just going to be average tenants where there's some work involved and you'll have an occasional issue, but overall they are okay. Obviously, you want the top 10%. Once you get them, treat them really well, which goes back to what I already mentioned: Keep the property in good shape, check the fire detectors, make necessary repairs, and you'll have happy tenants. And while you do not want to get too close to them socially, if you get that gem of a tenant, you might want to keep him happy with little kind gestures. For instance, send them a birthday card or a Christmas card, or one on the anniversary of their lease. With really good tenants, you may even include a $5 (or so) gift certificate to a coffee shop in his neighbourhood. In other words, do what you must to keep your tenant. It's always cheaper to keep the customers you have than to find new ones – and the next one may not be as good.

Another reason to stay on your tenant's good side is the potential snowball effect. In other words, if he ever moves out, you want him to tell everyone what a great landlord you are, rather than badmouth you and tarnish your reputation in the community. A good word here and there will make it that much easier to find a new tenant, or maybe the old one can recommend someone – all because you've been a terrific landlord. Plus, he will probably leave the property in a much better condition if he likes you. You certainly don't want the tenant leaving piles of trash and damages in his wake, do you?

I can tell you from my own experience that I've had tenants who stayed with me because we got along so well; as a matter of fact, they stayed even though I charged them $50 - $75 above the market rate for rent.

However, having said all that, I want to stress again that by a 'good relationship' I don't mean you should be buddies and hang out together. No. But there's no reason why you shouldn't be polite, fair, and respectful toward the tenant.

You only have one tenant right now, but hopefully in the future you will own multiple properties. If tenants start comparing notes and realize that you treat one of them better than the others, or that you are chummy with one but not the rest, there will be resentment. So don't play favourites – be nice to everyone.

Ouch, you have a tenant from hell

You have followed all the common-sense rules outlined above, but somehow you now have a really bad tenant. He is consistently late with the rent and it grates on your nerves.

What do you do? Do you let it slip and give him a few days leeway?

Absolutely not. I don't care if it's a sweet old lady who is baking you apple pies every month. Unless lightning has struck the bank or locusts attacked your town, tardiness should not be tolerated.

This is how you protect yourself: There's a document (in Ontario it's called an N4, I am not sure what it's called in the other provinces) that tells the renter he missed his rent and has 14 days to pay it, after which time you will go to court to apply for eviction. If the tenant pays up within 14 days, the document gets filed and that's the end of the story. The problem is that if you don't act immediately – in other words, present the document to the tenant on the day after the rent was supposed to be paid, you are only delaying the rent collection. Act immediately.

If you are dealing with that sweet little old lady and you want to proceed gently, don't mail the document to her or slide it under the door. Take it to her in person and explain that this is just standard procedure, but you must do this. Basically, you are covering your butt in case she doesn't pay up and you really do have to evict her (I know, it sounds heartless but you are not running a charity. This is a business). Be consistent and don't get sucked in by this sweet old woman because she'll learn to manipulate you.

Whether it's a late rent or excessive noise sparking complaints from the neighbours, document everything to the nth degree, because problem tenants don't have moments of epiphany when they realize they've been bad and change their ways. No. Experience tells you that these people will be chronic troublemakers, so in the end taking them to the tribunal might be the only course of action left to you. They might have the same idea too and plan on taking you to the Tribunal, so you'd better have all the legitimate documentation with you.

If you get the tenant's permission to videotape or photograph the property during your inspection, then you have the best kind of irrefutable proof should you have to go to court. But keep in mind that you can't – legally speaking – take photos or film without the tenant's authorization.

And while we are on the subject of bad tenants, an important point to bring up here is that illegal drug growing operations, commonly referred to as a 'Grow Op', are a big concern for landlords because that kind of activity can completely wreck and destroy your property. Since there is no insurance against tenants growing illegal drugs in your rental unit, you will be liable for the damage incurred. Therefore, I strongly recommend that you have a clause in your rental agreement giving you the right – not the obligation, but the right – to inspect the property monthly. You are probably not going to do it that often, but grow op guys tend to avoid renting those kinds of properties since they don't want anyone checking up on them.

I mentioned earlier that you should go in twice a year to do the physical inspection, but that timeline still leaves lots of time for a 'Grow Op' to operate in between. I am going to suggest that you do another inspection (smoke detector) twice a year as well, so now you are going to be on the premises at least four times a year. But, if suspicions arise, drop in monthly.

Let's hope you won't encounter this kind of a drastic situation too often – or ever!

Notes & Thoughts!

CHAPTER 9

HOW TO BUY AS MUCH REAL ESTATE AS YOU WANT

With none of your own money

The number one question I get when I speak at events is, "How can an investor buy property with none of his own money? Is this really possible?"

Yes, it is, but there's a caveat. You can purchase properties without investing a cent of your *own* money, but you still need to come up with someone's funds – be it a bank or private financing. So one of the most important lessons you will learn as you expand your knowledge of this field is who to deal with and how to go about setting up financing.

Okay, so now you are a landlord, have several months of (hopefully positive) experience managing your property, and feel ready to kick it up to the next level. However, you used up all your money for the down payment for that first property. Do you have to wait and save up for the down payment on your next investment?

Absolutely not. Let me explain with the following example: Let's say the house you bought was $200,000, and you put $50,000 of your own money into that deal, while the bank loaned you the remaining $150,000. Six months later you find another deal you want to jump on, but you need another $50,000 to put down. What are you going to do? You have two options: One is you can find a partner who will give you $50,000, buy that property, and split the profits in half.

Your second option is to remember that you have $50,000 equity in your first property. What if you were to borrow money against the first property in the form of a second mortgage, take that equity and apply it to your next purchase? If that's what you decide to do, you can go to another investor who is looking to earn 7%-10% on his investment and may be willing to lend you $50,000, and then register it as a second mortgage on your first property. Then you can take that $50,000 and apply it to another property purchase.

This would be a sweet deal because you would own 100% of that second property as well. And now you know that you don't have to put down $50,000 of your own money for each real estate purchase. In fact, you are able to put down as little as 20% without having to use insurance like CMHC or as little as 5% down if you choose to use insurance on these kinds of deals anyhow. So definitely use the leverage you already have on the first house, and get a second mortgage on there to buy your next property. But once you get going, you will probably want to look at having partners. Don't give in to the old 'lone wolf' mentality where you want to try and do everything yourself. Learn that leveraging other people for experience or money is the quickest way to create wealth.

This is a useful point for you to keep in mind because a lot of real estate investors would love to purchase more properties, but don't, because they believe – mistakenly, of course – that they must save up for the down payment. But, as demonstrated above, smart investors look for other options, such as getting a partner. Even though with another investor involved, you will only keep 10% of the profits, keep in mind that if you do 10 deals like that, in the end you will have a free property for yourself. In other words, put together 10 deals giving you 10% return each, and the tenth one will be all yours, with 100% of the profits going to you.

However, a 50/50 split is more common, so you only have to do two deals to get one free property. Now, you may be wondering how to get a partner, someone willing to put up the down payment. Why would someone want to do that anyway?

Well, it may be a person who would love to own a piece of property but has no knowledge of real estate, or perhaps no time to go through all the processes involved in purchasing a property. Look among the people you know and deal with regularly, professionals who service you, or maybe friends and family members. One of them might be willing to advance the funds against a guaranteed and quick return of 8%-10% on their investment. So becoming an expert in real estate will work to your advantage; the more knowledge and experience you bring to the table, the harder you are willing to work finding tenants and managing the property, the easier it will be to attract investors. At the end of the day, this is a win-win situation for all involved.

Another thing you should know – if you don't already – is that in Canada there is a retirement savings plan called the RRSP (Registered Retirement Savings Plan). Most people don't know that they can invest their personal RRSPs in real estate through a self-directed fund. What I mean is that you (or your investor) can take these funds out of the market and instead of earning only 3% in a GIC (Guaranteed Investment Certificate), get a much higher rate of 10-12%, by self-directing your investment into real estate.

Do as the wealthy do

If you want to make loads of cash in real estate, follow the lead of successful investors. Look at *Canadian Rich Dad* Darren Weeks. Look at others who started out with just one house and now own multiple properties.

Your first thought probably is, "Geez, this guy must be a multi-millionaire! How else could he afford to purchase all these properties?"

Well, now you know better. Chances are, all these wealthy investors started out slowly and modestly, but then they learned how to grow and expand their businesses. Basically, they learned what we had just talked about here. Use partners, use other people's money, use leverage. You can be as sure as night is dark that no established, successful investor – myself included – used their own money for the down payment on each of the properties they own.

Speaking for myself, I had nothing but my house when I started building this business; other people started with even less. It's not where you start that counts, it's where you end up.

Okay, so you now know that with real estate, the return on your investment is hefty. You have no money of your own in the deal, and you are getting cash flow, appreciation, depreciation, and all the other profit centre benefits. That's a huge leverage that's creating money out of thin air.

By the way, it's extremely important for you as an investor just getting started, to know how the ROI is calculated. If you want to attract more of other people's money, you have to understand the concepts and the terminology so that you can teach your investors what they can gain out of this partnership. Quite simply, the more people you teach and the more willing they are to put up funds, the more money you will make.

I speak here from a personal experience of dealing with investors and offering them great opportunities. As a matter of fact, I commonly refer to myself as a farmer who plants seeds. The more seeds I plant, the more opportunities will present themselves to me (basically, it's another take on 'you reap what you sow'). Realistically speaking, not all of these relationships will turn out to be prosperous, but I feel good about helping people plant those seeds, all the while hoping that one day they will turn around and invest with me, or give me a hand up or a reference.

This is why the importance of networking should not be underestimated. When I first started in this industry, I was totally intimidated by the word 'network' because I don't consider myself an outgoing person. What I quickly learned, however, was that networking is easily connected to teaching, and by teaching, which I love to do, I am creating a huge network of money.

So even if you are not a very gregarious person, you can still find networking beneficial. You don't have to hand your card to every person in the room – that's a total misconception. Your goal, when going to any kind of activity, should be to meet, connect, and start a relationship with just one person. Who knows, he or she may have over 5000 people in their database. See why it's so essential to network?

I'd like to convey one more point about seeking out other people's money. Although I personally prefer to work with a single investor, there's no law that says you have to limit yourself to just one partner. If you need $50,000 for a down payment, you might want to split it up among three people at just under $17,000 each. The advantage of this particular approach is that you can break one big sum into three smaller ones, which might be more manageable for some people. So there are lots of options for you to mull over.

Whichever way you look at it (and regardless of how many investors you are working with), it is extremely important to have good relationships with these people. You really want to treat these people well, and one way to do that is to give them an above average rate of return on their investment. Right now interest rates are very low, so if you are offering somebody a rate of return of 10% guaranteed, that's a very attractive deal. And when you decide to sell, each investor shares in the profits. If you do that, word will get around and pretty soon you will have more money chasing after you than there are available deals. That's one 'problem' everyone should have!

Notes & Thoughts!

CHAPTER 10

CREATIVE REAL ESTATE STRATEGIES – LEASE OPTIONS

Now that you have some experience as a real estate investor, know the ropes, and are on the lookout for more deals, it's time to get creative.

Say there are various opportunities coming your way but you are looking only at buy and hold possibilities. If that's your MO, you are leaving a lot of different opportunities on the table and you are losing a lot of money.

There are lots of creative ways of investing in real estate, and this book would not be complete if I didn't show you some of these strategies. Let's focus on what I consider to be the most creative one of all – the lease options.

When I am mentoring a young couple interested in getting into the real estate game, quite often their belief is that real estate is going to allow them to get rich quick. Clearly, the buy and hold strategy we have discussed in this book, where you purchase your first property as a long-term investment, is not going to make you wealthy overnight. However, there are many other strategies and opportunities to generate quicker cash flow. Once you become more seasoned in this business, you will learn to recognize these opportunities.

When I sit down with a couple for the first time, I explain the concept of lease options to them. Their eyes keep getting bigger and bigger, because the opportunity to make a lot of money in a short period of time can be phenomenal. It can replace their income very easily if they focus on doing just lease options. By 'focus' I mean work hard at it, but when you do, you will have a creative way to make quick money, or increase the cash flow on your existing properties. If you own just one single-family home that generates income, you could apply the concept of a lease option to that property as well, and improve your cash flow by several hundred dollars a month, typically within one to two years. We are looking at a chunk of money upfront, a significantly higher cash flow per month, and then another chunk of cash at the end – three main profit centres in all.

Let's walk through how I do a lease option. Typically, my lease options are three-year terms. By the way, another term for the lease option is 'rent to own', so that might sound more familiar to you.

There are two different types of lease options. The first one is called a sandwich lease option, where you rent a property from somebody with the option to buy it, and then you turn around and rent it to a third party with the option to buy it from you. As you can imagine, it can get pretty complicated. So let's focus here on a simpler model of lease options.

Who to deal with, who to avoid

The model I prefer is called a 'Purchase Lease Option'. This is how it works: I eliminate that first party or the original home owner, so there are only two people involved, myself and the client or the tenant. This program is mainly designed for people who are cash-rich but have bad credit. In other words, they have the money but don't have the credit to be able to qualify for a conventional mortgage.

Now, you may be wondering how someone can be cash-rich and credit-poor. A good example I like to use is a contractor like a roofer or some other trades person who has the opportunity to work for a lot of cash, which they don't report to CRA. Or perhaps they are able to expense a lot of their earnings, or their taxable income is too low to qualify for a conventional mortgage. In order to qualify for a mortgage they would have to show to the banks that they've got three years of consistent high income. So that's why it takes three years to get their income level up to where it should be. Then they can go to the bank and get a conventional mortgage for the purchase of the house.

Another example would be a new immigrant coming to this country. Quite often these folks have access to cash or they have a strong work ethic and access to jobs, so money is not a problem for them. However, since they have no credit history yet in this country, they can't qualify for a mortgage, so they'd have to wait for two or three years to build or develop that credit in order for the bank to lend them money.

Then you have young, new professionals, someone who just graduated from dental school and they are $150,000 or $250,000 in debt with student loans. Naturally, they aren't going to qualify for a mortgage right away, but since they have a high income, they can afford to make payments.

These are just a few examples of people who have money and no credit, but there are obviously many more out there. I think it's fair to estimate that 20% of those who can afford a mortgage don't qualify for one, so these are the folks who will be willing (and maybe even eager) to work with you.

A word of caution, however, in vetting the candidates, make sure they are financially stable (as described in above examples) and not people who have poor credit because they don't know how to manage money. Red flags should also go up in your head when dealing with people who had filed for bankruptcy. If they filed as a result of a marital breakup or a similar scenario that ruined their credit, but are otherwise financially stable, that's fine. But if they went bankrupt because they haven't managed their funds properly, I'd stay away, UNLESS they come up with a big chunk of cash upfront. As long as they have the money for the deposit it's on them to make sure that they make their payment.

Personally, I operate with the idea that I don't set anybody up for failure, so they have to assure me that they will be able to succeed in this venture because I want it to be a win-win situation. Needless to say, I want to make sure that I am not on the losing end. So yes, I always require a deposit.

How this works

Let's walk through the steps of how we do a lease options deal. We start with an ad in the newspaper or maybe a customer approaches us from whatever marketing resource we put out there. They are interested in our program, so they fill out an application. We look at the application and if we feel that these people are worthy candidates, we will contact them and explain to them what the program is like and how it works in detail. Then, if they want to move forward, we will give them an idea as to how much of a house they can afford based upon the information they provide.

Say they can afford a $250,000 house based on the numbers they have provided. I will ask them if there is a particular house or a particular neighbourhood they are interested in. I will look at the listings they bring me and pick one of them. I tell the clients they can go take a look at it with my real estate agent, and if we like the house we will make an offer to purchase it on the client's behalf. I will then own the house and rent it to the client with an option to purchase it from me three years down the road. So if the present market value of that house is $250,000, we are going to appreciate it by 5% a year.

Here's how I crunch the numbers: The market value is $250,000, and I will then add a 5% annual appreciation or rounded to a total of 15% of $250,000 ($250000 x 15%) which is $37,500 on top of that, so I am going to sell it to them in three years for $287,000. If they wait for three years before they can qualify to buy that same house, they are going to be paying $287,000 because markets would go up anyhow. The clients realize that and they are in agreement with that spread. What they don't know is how much I end up paying for the house. The market value is $250,000, but you know you should never pay the asking price, right? Let's say I bought that house for $240,000, so now I've got a spread of $47,000. That's my approximate profit in that particular deal.

Now, let's talk about rent, and again, these are just ballpark figures. Say the fair market rent is $1200 a month, but I am going to charge them $1500. That additional $300 I will credit back to them at the end of the three years, assuming they buy the house. If they don't buy, I keep that $300 a month as profit. On top of that, my expenses for that house are $1000 per month (mortgage payment, insurance and taxes), so I have another $200 a month profit in there; in total I have $500 a month cash flow coming to me, $300 of which I will potentially have to give back. Of course, I also asked for a deposit of at least 5%, so I am looking at approximately $12,000 cash when I create the deal. Will I take less? Sometimes. More? Definitely.

Now, let's say the client can't come up with the cash but is offering you something valuable as collateral – perhaps an expensive car or an antique piece of furniture. Should you accept? If you feel it's a fair exchange, you can consider it, but cash is definitely king.

Speaking of money for the down payment – I don't care where it comes from or how they get it (as long as it is legal) – they are ultimately responsible for paying it back if they need to borrow it from a friend or family member. After all, you are in it for profit, not just the kicks. Remember, this is a business. I now have $500 a month profit coming in, $300 of which I have to give back, as well as a $12,000 deposit that I have to potentially give back at the end of the term as well.

Actually, I don't really give it back to them at the end, my lawyer will reduce my profit by the amount of the credits when the deal is closed at the end of the term. So the day I receive the deposit and monthly credits I get to spend that money – it's my money now because it's non-refundable. If they fail to fulfill their commitments, they lose that $12,000, plus their credits. If they fail to complete the deal after two years and they walk away from it, I now have $7200 in credits ($300/mth x 24mths), plus a $12,000 deposit. I can discount that house by $19,000, sell it, and still get out of the deal and make a little bit of money, but that's the worst-case scenario. Or I can turn around and say, "Well, that was a good deal," and then find somebody else as a rent to own client. Another possibility open to me is that I can put a tenant in and just rent the house out and because I had the previous tenant pay down so much of the cost, the property will have a positive cash flow. So yes, your options are wide open.

The profitability factor

Say you want to quit your job and replace the income you would lose just with lease options. If you are earning $40,000 a year at your job, how many of these kinds of deals would you have to do a year to replace your current income?

Let's see, if you are collecting $10,000 deposits, you only have to do four deals a year.

So even if the deposits are your only source of income, you will have a much better lifestyle running single-family home lease options, and it's not a lot of work once you get the systems down.

Going back to the example where we had a $250,000 house, I would buy it for $240,000, have a mortgage for $200,000 from the bank, and I'd have to put in $40,000 cash. Once the deal closes, I would go to my investor(s) and offer them an opportunity to invest at 10% through their RRSP to put a second mortgage on that property. My investor is extremely happy because he is making $4000 a year – certainly more than the current going rate – so over the course of three years, I am going to pay him $12,000 in interest. I make a total profit of $47,000, pay my investor $12,000, so that means I have a $35,000 profit from that deal over a three-year period, with none of my money in it. Nice, isn't it?

And you know what's even nicer than that? Do four of those deals a year and you can laugh all the way to the bank.

Keep in mind, however, that we are talking about a three-year time frame, so you have to be consistent in replacing the deal. But as long as you keep replenishing, the cash flow that you can generate from this business is truly amazing.

As you can see, the lease option is another valuable tool in your toolbox of real estate goodies. You want to keep buying and holding those other properties, so in 20 years, when you are ready to retire, everything is paid off, and you have the cash flow and the equity.

But in the meantime, if you want to quit your job and be a full-time real estate investor, this is just one way to generate income.

It is also an excellent way to liquidate your single-family homes once you are no longer a novice investor and ready to move on to greater things. Two years down the road, you graduate to the big league and start buying the triplexes, the fourplexes, whatever. What do you do with the single-family homes? Do you sell them or do you go with a lease option? If you hold on to the property for another three years, you increase your profit margins by a tremendous amount and get out of the deal at the same time. So it's another exit strategy and another alternative to increase the value on a single-family home.

Another creative real estate deal is assigning deals. What this means is that you find a great deal, tie it up with an offer to purchase ASAP, and then assign the deal to another buyer. Basically, you negotiate a great deal, get all of your 'subject to' clauses in there, and then take that deal to your investment club and tell everyone that you have an opportunity to buy this property, and you are passing this contract/opportunity on to others. In effect, you are not selling the property; you are selling the contract. Somebody will give you X amount of dollars for that contract or the right to have that contract, but it's crucial that in the body of the contract you put a clause giving you the opportunity or permission to assign that contract to another purchaser. There is more to this, so you definitely need to seek some legal advice before attempting any of these strategies. These strategies are being mentioned here for the sole purpose of introducing the concepts and options available to investors.

Investing in real estate has been a life altering experience for me; it has provided me with the opportunity to not only change my own personal lifestyle for the better, but also those of others around me. I am passionate about helping others learn how to do what I have already accomplished.

I hope that in reading this book you have learned something. I hope that I have ignited a passion within you to not only learn and grow, but to invest in real estate. I also hope that you won't just stop here. If you are intrigued by what you have learned in this book, keep searching. There is much more to learn. There are many great and exciting opportunities out there for the taking.

****

In the beginning of this book, we promised to walk you through the ins and outs of real estate investing, giving you valuable tips, advice and fair warnings. We hope we have accomplished that goal, and that you now feel empowered to become an investor yourself.

Go forth and multiply (your real estate holdings).

Notes & Thoughts!

All The Best

K B

Creative Real Estate Investing for Canadian$

How to buy your very first investment property
- EVEN IF YOU HAVE NO MONEY

By Ken Beaton
With Dave Dubeau

Library and Archives Canada Cataloguing in Publication

Beaton, Ken, 1959-

Creative real estate investing for Canadians : how to buy your very first investment property, even if you have no money / Ken Beaton, Dave Dubeau.

ISBN 978-0-9783090-5-3

1. Real estate investment--Canada. I. Dubeau, Dave, 1968- II. Title.

HD1382.5.B416 2010 332.63'240971 C2010-900001-3

Illustrations by David Allred Studios
Cover and Graphic Design by Webgrity

April Dew Publishing Inc
202 - 15388 24 Ave.
Surrey, BC, V4A 2J2
www.aprildew.com